Michael Kingscote

Cons.M.B.A.P.S. Dip.Para.Psycol

Beyond Faith

To Yvonne and Brian,
all the best from the
author. Michael Kingscote

God Bless!

First published in Great Britain in 2009 by Manor Creative Publishing

ISBN 978-0-9561711-2-2

Printed and bound by Manor Creative Ltd, 7 & 8 Edison Road, Eastbourne, BN23 6PT
www.manorcreative.com

Acknowledgments

There are a lot of people I need to thank for their help and kindness.

Firstly of course Kim, for her love and understanding.

Colin and Cindy for travelling around with me and taking tickets.

Charlotte, Ashley and Natasha for combined computer and tea making skills. Gemmaine for the glamour! And Jean and John Shea the Inlaws!

Mike and Betty Occleshaw for the wonderful friendship .

Also: John Briggs, Nathan, Fran Harper, Robin Lown, Sharon Williams, David Harrison Derek Robinson Keith Charles.

And a special thanks to Steve and Jenny Grist, and Jonathon Wilson.

I would also like to thank everyone at Manor creative for all the help and kindness. Not just now but over the years.

BEYOND FAITH

Introduction

THE MOTIVATION to write this account doesn't come just from the 20 years that I have worked as a medium, but from a lifetime devoted to searching for the truth behind life and its meaning, and the possibilities that surround post mortem survival. It is only now that I can sit down and with 100% confidence and attempt to offer definitive answers to questions that each and every one of us will find ourselves asking at one stage or another through our lives.

"Is there truly a life after death?" If so, "where do I go?" "What does it feel like on the other side?" "Is there such a thing as reincarnation?" "How does religion and faith sit with scientific scrutiny?...."

These are all questions that I have attempted to tackle, and yes to positive conclusion as regards the answers, based not on faith, but on known and scientific facts. I hope that I have shown no bias because I am a medium, but I like to think that I am fair minded in evaluating all evidence of this nature.

The American medium John Edwards last did a series that was called "Cross country". In the titles you can hear him say, " How do I know...because I do". For me this is not adequate when faced with a strong brigade of skeptics whose only motivation seems to be to destroy belief. They seem so divorced from the humanity of what genuine mediumship is all about and I have to question their motives as much as they question ours.

So what I am saying is that the evidence I am attempting to produce is not based entirely on mediumship experiences, (which most books of this type are), but on the results of scientific experiments, done by well documented scientists, and myself with pictorial evidence gathered over the last couple of years.

It is true to say that I am of course not a scientist. All I have ever done in this regard is a diploma course in Parapsychology, which in itself was a fascinating experience. But where I offer photographs as evidence, I have made the selections based on what I know scientists have looked for and studied in similar pictures.

So not a lot qualifies me to have the audacity to attempt to solves mankind's search for truth. Only the fact that this has been a life times pursuit. A lifetime of trying to sort the wheat from the chaff as it were. As I said, I am aware that as a sensitive, I may be biased as to what is and isn't evidence.

If I was to hear a disembodied voice in my head, and that voice states a name that happens to correspond to the person whom I am with during the course of a reading, then I would regard that as part evidence of life after death.

That is of course what mediumship is and what it is supposed to be about. Establishing proof that A, a particular loved one is still a conscious being after death, and consequently B, that there is therefore life after death. Everytime I step out onto a platform or stage this is the soul purpose of doing what I do!

However, ….and here is the shocker,… I have had to alter my perspective! I have to now suggest that demonstrations of this kind are best suited to those who have already opened their minds to this process. The reason being that there are so many alternative explanations for what we do from magicians, illusionists, and psychologists, that real and genuine mediumship is lost in all these attempts to "expose" this as nonsense. Even sprouting websites like "Badpsychics.com" for example.

Derren Brown is a self confessed non-psychic medium, who at first appears to have the ability to control and influence the mind. In truth I feel that many of his antics are re-runs of parlor tricks, though done exceptionally well, and he is perhaps the most talented in his field.

Derren can do what I do. He has traveled the world doing platform demonstrations of mediumship that is often better than I have seen in some churches. His demonstrations are flawless and very evidential. However at the end he then drops the bomb shell that he is not a medium, and has no psychic ability, and that there is no truth in any of this!

In fact what he has just done is replicate a mediumship demonstration, and validated loved ones of people in the audience, lifting them up and giving them hope, then dropped them back down to earth with a huge bang!

His explanation is that he needs to highlight the truth and expose this fraud. (And this is regardless of any scientific scrutiny).

The fact that he can do this does however means that an alternate explanation is demonstrated from the skeptical community of our work. I know that when I do this I link to spirit, and I know what I see and hear, but because of this I have to question whether it is good enough to be considered proof or evidence of survival except to the converted.

This is why I have felt that this book is overdue, and with it hope to restore the balance back in favour of the medium.

The one person I have little time for is the so-called amazing "James Randi". His explanation for mediumship is both comical and highly amusing. On prime time television he suggested that they would send out a team to people's houses researched from names on pre-sold tickets to look through windows in order to gain information about that person. He actually did this himself to prove it can be done.

This in itself is a ridiculous notion. Many centers don't sell tickets up front anyway. Can you imagine someone like Steve Holbrook, the Wakefield medium, trying to send research teams out for what is very often up to five demonstrations a week? I think not.

I must confess though I have also seen some rubbish demonstrations at churches that could easily add weight to the skeptics. Sometimes I have felt like walking out. And it's always these people that seem to want to push themselves the most.

So the bottom line is simply that what Derren Brown does is impressive, but just because he can replicate the work of a medium, alternate explanation for this process compromises this in terms of actual evidence. However what Derren does in no way disproves mediumship. Copying a medium using mind tricks in no way proves or disproves whether the mind and brain are two separate entities.

This applies also to cold reading techniques. This is where the medium is said to convey messages via guesswork and body language and initiating prompts from the sitter. The fact that this practice exists does not invalidate the possibility that at a particular time, an alternate consciousness might in some way be able to affect the mind, or join with it in some capacity.

Finding out if this is at all possible, or happens at some stage during the course of mediumship is down to science, not the medium or the illusionist.

CHAPTER ONE

"Who Am I?"

FROM THE moment I picked up the pen to write this, sitting in the back of "Wendy" the fiat Doblo, (which, containing beds, cooker, and chairs, has also been like a home to me), I didn't want to do just another collection of anecdotes, which so many mediums often press on us when writing a book.

That's not to say I didn't have any. I also have case histories, which go back over twenty years now, including personal experiences relating to the paranormal, and the readings that I have done.

The anecdotal biography is something I may well want to tackle, and have thought about it after reading the books by the late Doris Stokes. For now it is important to me to be able to offer something that might just have enough credibility to turn the objective skeptic.

It is however important that you know the basics appertaining to my background in order to understand where I am coming from and how I have arrived at the conclusions that I have. So here is my world, in a mini, pint sized version lasting just the one chapter that hopefully won't send you to sleep.

I have lost track of how many times over the years I have began the explanation of what I do with the words "Ladies and gentleman, I hear voices!", and for whatever reason, it would always result in sniggers from somewhere in the audience.

I only started doing platform/theatre demonstrations in 2000. Rules change as they do, and up until that point I had been a spiritual healer. The law changing meant you now had to be registered with a particular governing body and hold relevant paperwork. This is very much what happened in the April of 2008 regarding mediumship, which in itself is a good thing. Despite this, I have to say I still hear a lot about people working in this field or offering invalidated messages without such affiliations, qualifications or indeed much ability at all!

So this was why I wanted to become a working medium as oppose to being a healer. This would have meant starting from the beginning again with a supervisor, despite healing since the age 19. I had heard voices and seen things while healing, and this was why at the time I felt I would be able to offer these messages as proof of post mortem survival. I Must admit I didn't sit in a circle, but was able to reach a stage of development with the help and guidance of an amazing Clairaudiant and healer called Patience Denten, who was my guide and mentor on the earth plane until her passing over, which was some fifteen years ago now.

But to go back to the beginning, I would have been about six years old when all of this started. I had always been very sensitive and had always struggled with that, but that sensitivity seemed to hit me in a different way at the time.

I remember it well. My Mum and Dad had split when I was just three years old, so it was just Mum and I in a damp rambling old masoniette in St Leonard's Hastings. Water ran down the walls, which I suppose helped wash the mould away, and as a result of these conditions was also a sickly child, suffering a lot of illness. I always seemed to be rushed into hospital for some reason or another. Bronchitis, asthma, croup … all words that I never seemed to hear the end of.

It was during one such visit that I was placed in an oxygen tent. This would have been at the now closed Royal East Sussex in Hastings. I remember the nurses were all evidently fussing around while I screamed for my Mum! Things were so different in the NHS then. Parents were not allowed to stay. I remember thinking Mums been sent home so why Can't I be?

My Mum often recalled that night herself, having to walk home in a foot of snow, whilst listening to my pitiful cries in the distance! I always thought her version a little Mills and Boon, but there you go. Regardless of the flamboyant imagery, that was the way Hospitals were run then, and some would say for the better. Truthfully, I do not believe that something like MRSA would ever have been able to breed in those days.

I stared through the oxygen tent; light seemed to bounce off the sides. It was then I thought I saw what appeared to be a nun standing behind the nurses. She didn't seem to arrive at all, she just appeared! I saw nothing bad about her. Nothing that made me feel this wasn't right. It was just the fact that she was there that I found unnerving. Then, a moment later she was gone! A little later I found sleep, and that's all I really recall of the whole incident. I am quite sure that were it not for this strange occurrence, the whole memory of this hospital visit would have vanished along with countless other childhood memories.

For a long time I never really thought that much about it. It was years later that I came to realise that this "Nun" might not have been a Nun at all. The headdress I realize corresponded to what a nurse would have worn many years before during the period of the Great War.

This was to be just the beginning. I wasn't seeing or hearing things all over the place but when it happened it happened! I remember clearly being in bed and seeing an old lady dressed in black standing at the foot of it! These visits eventually became nightly occurrences, and left me in such a state that I would spend all day dreading the night.

Mum didn't really understand, and it was not long after these started that I found myself having to see a child psychologist in order to try and fathom out these night terrors. Some might say that seeing an old lady at the foot of your bed might be reason enough, but no, His explanation, as Mum told me years later, was that I was upset because Dad had left home.

Sometimes I heard her talk. On at least two occasions I heard her refer to me as "Teddy" or "Ted". These incidents, along with others too numerous to mention continued to dog my life until I was around 12 yeas old, which ironically was the time we moved from the house. I still had the odd "Episode" as it were, but tend to attribute this to the memory of what had happened.

I went to Christ Church School in St Leonard's which meant going to church three times a week, a Wednesday, Friday and a Sunday. I even sang in the choir, and through this and my faith, found peace. My religion taught me that God was indeed the true protector of us all, and that belief meant to me that nothing " Out of this world" could harm you if your faith was strong enough.

When other kids my age were into football and music and decorating their rooms in posters appropriate to these interests, I had decorated my room in crosses and statues and all manner of religious icons. They brought me comfort, and at the time offered me some protection from the memories of what had occurred.

As I got older these things were replaced by regular "Boy stuff" like Airfix kits and posters from my favorite thing then, "Planet of the apes". Eventually my visions and voices vanished, and as I hit secondary school I heard and saw nothing.

I did however remain strong in my religious convictions, with many long chats with the priests at church, often talking the sun down, but for me. There were always more questions than answers and I started to resign myself to the fact that perhaps this is what was meant to be.

The fabric of this belief did however remain intact, and I even joined a Christian union group whilst at school, which met every Wednesday and numbered around 10 members. Can you imagine such a group in schools these days???

By the time I started college age 16 studying graphics I was exploring new possibilities. I had read up on the supernatural/paranormal, as my personal experiences in my child hood seem to hit on a few raw nerves within that area. However there was a very strange moment that I feel is worthy of mention, and this is despite the fact I was no longer going to church on a regular basis.

During a lecture, a good friend of mine called Phil had spoken about Christianity, saying that it was nothing special and just a religion.

Without anything to back me up, my reaction was suprisingly defensive of what I had regarded as my old faith. In fact I remember shouting "Christianity is not just a religion, it's a fact, it's the truth"! I remember a similar incident in conversation with my Dad, an atheist. I would not be told otherwise, and yet, sadly I had no real argument to back this up other than say, the Bible, and most scholars would easily question as to whether this could possibly be enough. (I will talk more about this later).

Retrospectively I now liken this to what I term "A.D.S" Auto defense syndrome, which is where you believe something so much that it is engrained in you, and you

9

will defend it to your last breath whether or not the evidence exists that you are right. This is seen in nearly all religions, and causes this blindness to exist when faced with real evidence that contradicts what you want to be true. Hence the huge clashes between science, theology and religion.

A.D.S is not unique to religion. I have seen a parapsychologist that seems to possess this syndrome too. There is one that I can think of but it would be far to invidious to mention his name, but he will not move from his stance that all things have a rational explanation despite any amount of growing evidence to the contrary.

I suppose when I was 19 my mind kind of "Imploded" Into this New World of separate consciousness. I was literally sucked back into it because of someone I was seeing at the time. She had become ill, and naturally I wanted to help. However I noticed something very strange about this illness. Many of the symptoms seemed to be identical to the feelings I had when I had gone through all those issues as a child.

I had met, let s call her "Heather", when I was, as I said 19. I had just finished college and we were enjoying, what's that quaint old-fashioned word? Courtship.

Without going into too much detail, after about six months of seeing each other, she started to complain of dizziness, and symptoms similar to my own. The technical term I now understand to be "Sleep paralysis". I decided to seek out a spiritual healer because I recognised this as being a little more than just high blood pressure.!!!

In some ways I hoped I was wrong. A friend with whom I had been at college introduced me to his aunt. A healer caller Valarie Fraser, who then sent me on to the lady who, was to become my teacher and mentor, Patience Denten.

Patience was a healer with remarkable Clairaudiant abilities, who for me proved her abilities time and time again. From her little house in Bexhill, I personally witnessed all manor of illness cured from cancer to serious heart conditions, and it was with her I learned to "Listen" to those disembodied voices that were to become such an important part of my life.

Patience introduced me to the concept of having spirit guides, and how these extraneous intelligencies interact with us on a daily basis once we have provided permission for them to do so. After all freewill is the second most powerful force in the universe next to God, and nothing is allowed to interfere with it.

Heather made a steady recovery, but I soon began to see that this was a way to introduce me to Patience and the world of spirit. Maybe this was never about her after all?

However this book is written as a factual account, so with this in mind I am not going to talk about spirit guides and what really are only beliefs due to the lack of concrete scientific cooberation. So from 1983 to 2000 I was a healer, who when healing sometimes heard voices, saw things and gave messages!

A lady called Peggy came to see me who had quite bad arthritis. During her 40 minute healing session I kept getting the impression of the name "Frank". After I asked her if she was familiar with this name and she became very emotional, telling me it was the name of her late husband.

" Do you have a caravan or a caravan park connection, 'cause this is what I keep seeing" I said to her. " We owned a caravan park… I still do" she answered.

"And I can hear him now, and he keeps saying about the money stashed in the loft"

"Money in the loft" She replied "I don't know what that means"

After she said that my new found self-confidence waned somewhat so I left it. It was a week or so later that Peggy's friend Pat, whom I had worked with at the time told me that Peggy had become curious over what I has said and decided to check out the loft. Hidden away in a case was a large amount of money that she had not even known about.

My friend Liz was the family's hair dresser, (Not mine)! I remember once having a conversation about this, and other matters to do with spiritualism ,when all at once I became aware of a male energy within my consciousness. I did not get a name other than the word "Dad" as is sometimes the case as frustrating as this may be.

" I think I have your Dad with me" I said

"Oh yeah and what's that about" Liz replied a little cynically

" He is showing me what looks like a teddy with a Mexican hat and a Clint Eastwood style poncho on"

With this Liz turned a little pale "God that is amazing" she said

"So this is significant?" I asked, pushing her just a little

"Very she said, and was even able to produce a photograph of the exact image I had seen which was something very private between Liz and her late father. This was to be just the beginning.

The reason I have pulled a couple of personal anecdotes out of the hat is to illustrate why I felt confident that I might be able to do a reading or two from a platform. I knew at the time that in some way I was being prepared and by the year 2001 I was more than ready.

Already I had seen the law change with healers and knew it was only a matter of time when this had to happen with Mediums, it had to. There were far to many quacks, charlatans and moneymakers that seemed to be able to do what they liked and it had to stop, so I knew that if I were going to be a legitimate Medium, time was running out.

By one of those acts of synchronicity I was able to contact a brilliant man by the name of Brian Marland. A Medium who worked at the Claremont church. Normally Mediums there are booked a year a head, but there was a cancellation, and I had the chance to see what I could do.

The next Saturday there was hardly a seat unfilled as I made my way on to the platform all the time thinking "What are you doing Mike, your about to make a total Pratt of yourself"

I need not have worried, I remember it like it was yesterday. Whenever I work, (And I will talk about the process later) I start with like buzziness in my ear, which is like a message to say "We are here"! It's through that buzzing and the tone changes that the voices come.

I immediately linked to an elderly man at the front I got the impression that he was not a regular at this sort of thing and didn't really know what to expect. Little did he know that neither did I!

"I have a younger male in spirit, and he is asking to acknowledge the younger male this side of life, so I see them as being brothers" I said. That would mean that you have two sons, One here and one there!

"Oh no" he said, I only have one son.

I repeated what I was getting, It stayed the same and did not vary at all. I really didn't understand why he said no, although I realise now there can be linguistic misunderstandings, and I don't always explain it simply. At that time I remember I just wanted to get down.

"So you just have the one son?" I said back to him.

"Yes" he answered ""Just one son. The other one's dead!

In a moment I had learned just how tolerant in some cases I was going to have to be. Then it was all over. The whole experience seemed to pass in a flash. I was excited but not sure how I had done as I had in the past had so little experience with platform work.

Its interesting to note that during the course of my work I developed with my guides a system of seeing a light to the head, to the side or to the bottom, which meant, to the top, parent, grand parent, or guardian. To the side brother/sister or contemporary, or below, child or younger member of the family. Years later TV Medium John Edward was on the TV doing exactly the same thing, and the cheek of it, using what I had always seen as being my own symbols. Also I used to say that if someone didn't get a message from that platform its like going to a birthday party but its just not your birthday, but you get a piece of cake! I heard him use something similar to this too.

Brian called me the next day and booked me nine demonstrations for the next year. I suppose you can say that it went rather well. Within one month I was getting calls from all over, and I was now at last established.

The trouble with this work is that it will at some stage leave you out of pocket. If you do a divine service somewhere and only six people show, and they only take two quid in the collection you can hardly ask for your tenner petrol money can you!

Then there was White noise promotions LTD! In 2006 to legitimise what I was doing, now outside of churches, I set up white noise promotions, A company, which was designed to make it all happen easier. But with each dem' we were really badly out of pocket, and it folded in under a year. It was my fault. I did not want to make money just cover the costs, and the result speaks for itself.

There was nothing left after hiring the venue and advertising. And we quickly fell into a minus balance on every venue we did, despite some of them being full houses. This was because we had to cover the bad nights. So for example in one case, Dover, we had a 500-seat theatre, two bar staff, and an usher, and only seven tickets sold.

This is why I was sad to receive an abusive text while I was in Crawley. I had just done a leaflet drop of 1000 + leaflets and was shattered. Kim forwarded me the text message as it had gone to her phone. It was apparently from a church member.

It read "Come to your local spiritualist church. We don't charge, or rip people off. Healing and clairvoyance is free, get a proper job, and fund your spiritual work from it like we do"

Well I had a proper job, and was doing just that. To date I had spent over £3000 from my job promoting spirituality. All I can say is that they can't be that good if they didn't know it.

It's a shame those so called Crawley spiritualists didn't want to get to know me. They would have found that many of my nights were for Charity.

Not long after white noise died a natural death I was in Hastings down a place known as the "Bourne", and came across a Psychic fair. Many of these are money – making racketts, but these prices seemed very reasonable. I happened to notice a name on the list of readers that was familiar to me, that of "Robin Lown".

Robin had been on Big brothers little brother, but I remembered him best as a palm reader on "The paranormal world of Paul Mckenna" and the TV series Mystic challenge. I remember his name because he had been good. One of the best along with a card reader called Inbaal, who was amazing and mediums Ronnie Buckingham and Keith Wade.

So when I saw Robins name on the board I decided I wanted a reading. Up until then the only person I had asked to read me was Inbaal as I trust her totally, and she has remained a good friend. I had myself often got psychic information by holding someone's hand, and wondered if this was what a palmist really does? Or if they're really was something weird and wonderful in all those lines. Being a Medium makes me open minded to any process, but the parapsychologist in me makes me want to know the truth.

I didn't think I would stand a chance of getting a reading so late in the day, but Robin agreed to hang back especially to see Kim and I.

The experience was life changing to say the least. I must confess to being a little star struck, but as soon as we walked into the room Robin perceived my spiritual nature and the work I do, which illustrated to me straight away that there was more to him than being just a palmist.

We talked the sun down and Robin asked me for my contact details which I was more than happy to give him.

"I'll call you," He said. "I have an idea" I really had no expectations from this, and in fact it was to be the best part of a year before I unexpectedly heard from him. At this particular time I was on the verge of closing white noise promotions down completely, mainly due to the poor ticket sales, and was far happier giving demonstrations for local charitys. Then, one night I was at Portland place spiritualist church for my very good friends Colin and Cindy Fuller (this church was and very often is packed out), and I had a surprise guest in the audience, a certain Mr Lown and Mystical promotions (what had been a similar company to my own), director Barry Wright.

I didn't let Robin remain in the shadows, electing to expose him from the platform, and welcome him publicly. Robin seemed comfortable in standing for the applause that he got. I now knew that this had to be a good night, and wanted more than nothing but to impress the well turned out Mr Lown. His last words to me were words that I never really expected to hear "I only work with the best, that means I'll be working with you"

Up until that time Colin and Cindy who ran the church took over a lot of the administration on white noise promotions and we traveled around doing demonstrations. Without Colin and Cindy I don't think I would have had the confidence to do what I do today. I would also have to talk about Mike and Betty Occleshaw, but they get a whole chapter in the section on "Tatiana" to themselves!

Colin took a lot of audio and video of my work .It was then that White noise died and Mystical promotions took over, and for a year I was managed by them.

Mystical promotions were already promoting Robin and I think I am right in saying, thought I would bring in bigger audiences, because you would also have the people interested in mediumship as well as those who like the psychic stuff, like palms, auras colours, runes etc.

Unfortunately what they didn't account for was the fact that no matter how well I did, the reputation of the Medium had been seriously tarnished by endless centers opening up and booking mediums who very often were unable to do what they claimed. If you run a center then you are under pressure to have a different medium often twice a week, and there just are not enough.

I don't want to sound cynical, but if you are working an audience of 200 + then you must produce something reasonable, or that is 200 people you have lost and will more than likely never step into a spiritualist church or center again! You must produce names, dates, places and lifetimes anecdotes.

So that's what was happening, especially in some churches. I see churches more now like the comedy store where people learn their art. So very often Mediums want to step out of that comfort zone, and are really not ready. I very often feel that these days its not about spirituality more about fame and being on most haunted, which is fine, but the most ambitious mediums seem divorced from the real reasons we are mediums. Not to be on the telly but to provide evidence of survival where possible, and more importantly comfort and support for the bereaved and those in difficulty. As for the ones who are on TV and known in that regard, its because they can do what it says on the bottle and very often didn't set out with that expectancy.

The point is when mystical promotions took over I did not generate the huge crowds that were expected. .

My first event with Robin however, was one that I organised, and was the very last one still using the white noise umbrella. Robin and I called ourselves "Connections"

I remember it well. I was in Bognor Regis at the time. I was booked into a community center the next week there, and Kim and I had just done a promotional leaflet drop. We were finding that 1000 leaflets usually only brought in 30 people or more. Despite this we had found this to be the most effective form of promotions. During surveys hardly anyone saw the expensive ads in the papers.

Whilst promoting my appearance in Bognor, the phone hardly rang at all for tickets. However it didn't stop for the Connections show which was the week after in Hastings at the Royal Victoria Hotel. In fact within hours it was sold out with all 100 available seats gone.

On the night of the Connections show Robin brought a projector which displayed your palm on a huge screen and as he read from selected audience members people became more intrigued by his art. We worked well together and bounced off each other very well. We chalked up a success, and felt very pleased that we were able to offer something that at first seemed to be an original combination.

Connections toured around for a year, but towards the end was again a huge financial loss that sadly saw the end of Mystical promotions as huge debt mounted from empty venues. I have a few ideas as to what was going wrong, but much of it on the surface appeared to be bad luck. One example was that we were at the Sallis Benney theatre in Brighton, and an arrangement had been made for tickets to be sold from the Brighton Dome, but I heard on that night that the Dome box office denied any knowledge of our event. Also it was on firework night. Kiss of death!

During that time we really enjoyed what we did, especially the radio. Robin and I appeared on BBC Southern counties with Mike Powell. I read on air for like three hours while Robin did palms from faxed photo copies.

In all that time I only had one person who could not take the message. Originally we were only supposed to be on for 30 minutes, but it was a huge success. This went out to something like a million listeners as it was extended to five counties.

The hardship was the restrictions the BBC place on talking about mediumship, and what you can include in a reading. I was shown an ethics manual, which was like War and Peace and Know that I broke the rules. Now they don't allow psychics and mediums on any more.

Mike Powell was impressed. In the pub after, I gave him an impromptu reading. All I can say is that he seemed impressed, especially as I was able to contact the one person on the other side that he said he had hoped to hear from.

We were also on local radio. We were booked into the Winter Gardens, which was a dinner event, and was sold out. To promote this event Robin and I went on Sovereign radio, and offered free tickets as competition prizes. It was decided that Robin would do a reading live on air, and broadcaster Sharon Williams joined us in the studio as his Guinea pig.

It went very well. I was not able to read Sharon myself on air, such was the sensitivity regarding mediumship. However off the air, I was already getting a link to a man in the spirit world, and I knew he desperately wanted to be known to her.

Eighteen months later, Sharon was to recall the incident in Look magazine published in the August of 2008. Sharon said…

> *He told me (Me) he had a message from a man who had a heart issue, and a very unusual problem with his foot. My heart swooped. My Dad had died three years earlier of aortic aneurysm. He also had an unusual growth on his heel. " He wants to tell you he is not angry with you for leaving the room" Michael continued, I was floored. When Dad collapsed at home I called an ambulance The paramedics needed to take blood, and because I'm squeamish. I left the room. At that moment he died and I felt horrendously guilty that I had not been there.*
>
> *Now hearing Michael s words I felt a huge relief. He also told me Dad was showing him roses. which puzzled me. Mum reminded me that we had thrown roses onto his coffin. It was uncanny, and there was no way he would have known. I was a stand in guest so he wouldn't have been able to research me.*
>
> *Michael's message was so healing When Dad died I felt very insecure. I was only 20 and had to take two months off work, but it took Michael's reading to really help me on.*
>
> *My relationship broke down, but I felt able to cope which wouldn't have been the case before meeting Michael.*

This was to be the start of a friendship. The next time I was on the radio it was after investigating the Eastbourne waterworks. I was asked to go down there after a clairvoyant night at a packed house down at the royal Victoria in Hastings.

A gentleman called Mark Wey told me of the paranormal problems there, but I will talk about that later in the chapter devoted to paranormal investigations.

I had been on air with Sharon, so asked her along to the next vigil, (The word used to describe a sort of ghost hunt) which was at the Mermaid in Bexhill. This yielded amazing results, and along with Ocean Bowling in Bexhill, and the Star Inn at Alfriston ranks as one of the top three best experiences of this kind.

The Mermaid stands out as being quiet unique, and clips from that night were broadcast on South east today. At one point Sharon had a glass fly at her, but again, this is another story best told later.

At the time of writing Sharon and I have worked together on several of these kind of investigations, and are waiting to hear if she will actually be presenting a programme called "Sussex Ghosts" with me somewhere in town We'll see.

So after a year the Connections shows came to a halt. At one point we had grown from Robin and I, to being four strong with amazing psychic and colour reader Caroline Small and psychic artist Ella Moonbridge, with whom I also worked separately on occasions.

Our last connections show was in Shoreham in the November of 2008, by then the format had run out of steam.

I have worked with quite a few Mediums over the years. Ann Gemaine, Marlene Woolgar, Sue and Leigh Smith to name a few. I eventually moved the Hastings venues from the Royal Victoria hotel to the High Beech hotel in Battle for two reasons. The first being that the audiences had grown to up to 200 plus for Hastings, and also, during a visit from Sue and Leigh Smith at the royal Vic, a member of staff was very rude, and to be quite honest, it was embarrassing in front of guests.

The last event at the High Beech at the time of writing was with a young medium called Sarah Jane Boden, whose abilities to link with spirit are quiet breathtaking. We had a crowd of 211, and made a good amount of money for the "mustard seed mission", a charity for eastern European children.

Sarah will one day be world wide, but needs to focus on her young family right now, and so can be elusive, but watch this space. She is very much like my favorite T.J.(Tracy) Higgs. It would be interesting to see them work together. You could almost imagine it falling into a good old cockney knees up half way through.

One of the other mediums I adore is Wakefield's Steve Holbrook. A really nice guy. I have often advised people to go and see him for his stage presence alone. He is a wonder to behold, let alone the remarkable evidence he produces. Like wise is "Psychic cop" Keith Charles, the original psychic cop and TV Medium. Keith plays it straight, and his no nonsense approach makes him probably one of the best Mediums in the world right now.

So you can imagine how flattered I was when he invited me to work with him at Wimbledon, at the church there. The very place that saw the likes of Doris

Stokes, Doris Collins, Coral Porge, Jesse Matthews, and the late great Gordon Higginson.

I got to meet the legend Derek Robinson too!

Sadly the evening was not one of my best as I was very nervous. In the back of my mind I knew that Keith was there, and I think it got to me. Keith has very high standards and firm opinions, and this was on my mind the whole time, but despite this I did ok, but ok for me is not good enough.

I am currently looking forward to the next three events booked with Keith and Ivan Lee. Namely in Hastings, Chatham and Wimbledon. At the time of writing I have not met Ivan but have heard great things about him.

So there it is. Of course I could write a biography on its own, I have enough personal experiences, but as I said right at the beginning, my aim is not to do that right now, but where possible to provide just the facts, and ensure that facts and fiction are kept totally separate. Science has conceded that the mind and body are separate. This is a "fact". This and other such "Facts" I intend to explore with you in the following chapters. As facts, I now no longer consider the arguments of the skeptics; after all we might just as well believe that the world is flat and the center of the universe.

I did a podcast for a guy in the states who calls himself the "Amateur scientist", who is a total skeptic, with a total skeptic following I answered every single question he threw at me, with an answer that was hopefully not only appropriate to my belief system, but has some form of scientific basis. At the end of it he said, "Michael Kingscote is a very nice guy, whom I just happen to disagree with about everything".

This is fair enough, but I got the impression he would swear the world was flat just to be opposite to me. (A.D.S, auto defense)?

When we spoke about Orbs, his opinion was of course that they were no more than dust, or camera flash etc. I mentioned that scientists like, Klaus Heinemann had disproved this, especially because of the speeds that real Orbs had been recorded at, sometimes in excess of 500 mile per hour, and often has comet like tails! They are also known to be only sensitive to the infa-red and ultra-violet ends of the spectrum, which would also disassociate them from many natural formations.

This was not accepted as viable at all. The fact that Heinemann was a NASA scientist held no water at all. So I put it to the test. When I spoke about an investigation into paranormal happenings that I was asked to do at the Eastbourne waterworks. I spoke about E.M.F.s (Electro magnetic fields), which is interesting because spirit produce natural fields of this nature. We can use a meter to pick up these fields and so hopefully bring about evidence of their being a presence that can be measured.

However E.M Fs can also be produced naturally, and can have a strange effect on the temporal lobe of the brain causing dizziness, nausea, paranoia, and the feelings of being watched and touched, in other words, all the things that you would feel if you thought you were being haunted! Except there is no ghost or spirit.

So I used this to test the water so to speak. I explained that I had measured a huge amount of natural E.M.F readings, which would effect people in exactly the way I have just described. I explained the cause of this energy was the huge network of underground cables over which they worked. In other words this was natural phenomena due to what we know to be NATURAL electric energy. His answer indicated that I had been trying to explain a paranormal happening, and I found that despite the fact that I was almost agreeing with him, he was disagreeing with me!

It was during a Connections show at the Sallis Benney theatre in Brighton with Robin that a man came up to me whose name I sadly can't recall.

He said that he was a magician and illusionist who had worked with the likes of Derren Brown and James Randi. I am sure you can imagine my guts turned over. He obviously noted the look on my face, because he said "Oh No, don't think we are all think like that. I know this is different, and I can tell that you are not trained in our ways. I just wanted you to know".

One night doing a ghost watch, and enjoying an evening with a small selected team. The evening was going very well and we were able to capture activity on our infa- red monitor.

Just then, a man came to the bar, a family member of one of my team. He was from Newcastle, and made it very clear very quickly that he had no time for all of this!

He started calling my team "Gullible", though I didn't bite. I didn't see the point. The down side is that as soon as he appeared and we had to sit listening to his voice, the energy disappeared, and stayed away all the time he was there. Nothing happened on camera. As soon as he was gone the activity resumed.

This just goes to show how the mind effects everything and that like attracts like. It was annoying, but interesting. What was all the more annoying was that I had paid for exclusive use of that bar, as he should not have been there anyway!

The same thing happened at the Red Stack playhouse in Bexhill. The first message went well, then these two girls came in, and were very cynical, shouting out, and making a noise. I had a terrible first half, and then they left during the interval, not before being given a refund. Once they had gone I was back on form. I wish it was not like this as it makes skepticism hard to deal with, but at the end of the day, it proves that skeptics are not our enemies, but their own!

Skepticism is based on nothing at all. It is a belief that has little to no knowledge. One parapsychologist at least I know would dispute this, but when you look for answers in the brain when they exist in a different place you will not find those answers.

I know of dozens of scientists that validate this work, and quantum physics alone sets about proving what we know to be true, that is that the mind and brain are not one and the same.

This itself would suggest that a skeptic is someone who has just not done their homework, and formulated an opinion without being in possession of all the facts. My northern friend I mentioned is one of these. Just like many of the people I have met in the print trade (My profession) over the years.

I always say we have to make a choice, and I would rather listen to what people like Klaus Heinemann, William Tiller, Peter Fenwick. Dave Fontana, Miceal Ledwith, who actually have a body of evidence to offer rather than Bob the builder, Taff from the chip shop or Dave the plasterer from up the road. It's your shout

This book is designed to be the final word, well, from me anyway.

CHAPTER TWO

"The nature of Quantum"

AT SOME stage we have to concede scientific reality. Were it not so we would never progress, and mankind would still be living in caves and hunting its food with spears!.

That said, sometimes looking at youth culture I have to ask myself if we aren't going backwards, but this is not the time for the soap box!

With this in mind it seems strange to me that even now, when presented with facts that have undergone scientific scrutiny, people are still inclined to put up a barrier or wall. We are in the west, the worse ones for that, and can only conclude that its because of the way we view our lives. Our love affair with materialism seems to be the one thing that has closed our minds to the waves of endless probabilities that could in fact change our lives for the better.

To be honest religion hasn't helped. We live in an age now where the church has come under close scrutiny, and that scientific, and historical evidence against the backdrop of orthodox religion is raising more questions than answers. The big question is therefore does this alter our faith? I would actually suggest not. The reasons for this will unfold in the following chapter on the nature of Quantum physics relating to proof of the afterlife.

In order to validate the after life the first thing we have to do in assessing the evidence is learn to think!

Going back a couple of years I had just finished doing a demonstration of Clairvoyance in Ashford, which is a good one or two hours drive from where I live, depending on traffic. As usual after such a demonstration I became ravenous.

I was with my partner (now wife) Kim, and we decided to stop off halfway in a coastal town called Rye, in the hope of finding somewhere to eat that was not too expensive (Fat chance of that)!

Time was getting on and we were up against the clock, as most places were starting to close. Unfortunately I failed to find the local chip shop if there was one, and made the mistake of going into a local bistro. I don't know why, but in my head I thought Bistro-Café, same sort of setup? I blame the seventies TV comedy Robins Nest for giving me the wrong idea!

So anyway, they found us a small table for two, and we started to unwind and reflect on the nights demonstration. (untill I got the bill at the end, and I wasn't quite so unwound anymore)! It didn't take long for Kim and I to realise that a man sitting on the next table in a party of four had recognised me from another demonstration, and must have commented on this to his companions. Inevitably this had sparked up a debate.

The two couples kept looking over, and the other male in a too loud not to be heard voice started saying things like ""Complete and utter rubbish" and " I cant believe you bought into that, people like that just feed off the vulnerable"

I felt Kim shuffle her feet uncomfortably under the table, as my reaction in situations like this tends to vary. I can switch off and just ignore them, but also, if I have had a bad day, or am over tired, or not had my Mars bar, I can also erupt like a huge volcano!

As it happens on this occasion I was too tired to bother and I just let him get on with it.

We heard the other mans wife say something like, "No, you really have to see what he does. It s all very real, but you have to experience it for yourself". Her husband whose recognition had sparked the debate in the first place had taken a back seat, which involved him just looking at the floor!

Then I heard " If we all lived on, there would be hundreds and billions of people since the world began, where would they all go? There wouldn't be enough room"

It was at this point I was glad I didn't bite. The stupidity of his logic managed to allow me to switch off. With that mentality it suddenly occurred to me that there was no way that I would ever be able to offer any evidence that he might have been able to take on board on the face of it.

So No, I didn't take the bait, and didn't get drawn in. He made a comment on the prices when I walked passed to go to the toilet, with the notion of getting my attention, but I just smiled, agreed with him and carried on. But lets look at this in hindsight. What might I have said?

How about Ok Mr, lets look at the planet "small" as it is in the universe, which I'm given to believe is a pretty big place, have you ever looked just that little bit further. The stars, the solar system, what then? Billions and billions of solar systems in the universe, in billions and billions of universes and what lies beyond that. Some sort of interstella cardboard box that holds it altogether ?

Then what lies outside of the box? Something must hold the box, that holds the box, that holds the box ??? Behold the miracle of infinity. So straight away, what we perceive as scientific reality is also embracing the paranormal, because here on Earth, our minds just are not capable of grasping the reality of infinity!

Had this man ever taken the time to sit back and think about that? Somehow I doubt it.

In some capacity I think we could call this A.D.S again. This is something you will hear me refer to again and again. A.D.S is also a cop out for people. A way of not having to accept the reality of possibilities. So Infinity is in fact the first of these realities or possibilities. By going into a form of denial I think it is a psychological way of not having to deal with them. The unknown is a scary place to be, and to go into denial is in itself a form of protection.

For hundreds and thousands of years, people have spoken about the process of "healing", and how the sick can be cured through some form of transferance of energy. Of course the skeptic will claim that healing is either a total illusion or the effect of Placebo, being a posh word for wishful thinking.

Experiments in the placebo effect have in the past yielded some very interesting effects. The main one that comes to mind is how in trials, a group of two dozen women with similar ailments where divided into two groups of two. One group was given specific medication targeting their ailments while the others were given chalk tablets.

Those who took the chalk tablets did just as well, if not better in some cases than their counterparts. For many this proved that the mind has an ability to trick you into thinking you are being made better when you are not, and therefore creates a strong case for placebo.

However, my pursuit for just the facts, has helped me to discover information regarding other tests that display a different result, and also to a degree, prove what I have always thought that those doing the tests have already made up their minds as to what the results are going to be!.

This was seen recently on TV when they tried to explain out of body experiances as a brain trick, or the usual "lack of oxygen in the brain as you pass over" senario. The test never at any time took into consideration the anecdotes that involved being able to describe another room that your body was not in, at the time of many of these episodes .

The other tests using healing tecniques deployed by spiritual healers and Reiki practitioners ETC. This time the results were conclusive, but in favour of healing, and not so much placebo. There was huge improvement, sometimes as much as 45% in days compared with those that did not receive healing. How did they rule out placebo? Because the healers never went near the patient. They used a process of absent or distant healing and the patients themselves did not know who was receiving the healing and who wasn't.

So already we are seeing that in some capacity, the mind is working "Outside" the confinements of the brain, in some way being the cause and effect of change. This capacity to effect change by thought alone is of course not a new idea.

In Washington DC, 4000 volunteers from 100 counties were assembled together. The purpose was a group meditation focused on the high crime rate in Washington. It was claimed that by the power of thought alone the crime rate could be reduced by as much as 25% The chief of police at the time was naturally very skeptical of such a claim, but when the event took place to his surprise, there was indeed literally a 25% drop in crime.

So already we are not only looking at the mind in some way working outside of the physical body, but seeing its effects and capabilities. But of course this ability is not a new discovery, but one that has been utalised and spoken of for literally thousands of years, which also provides a spring board for all those concepts regarding things like "Karma".

With this cause and effect process in mind, one of the names that has come to light is a certain Dr Masaru Emoto. Born in 1943 he is a graduate of the Yokohama Municipal University's department of humanities and sciences, and author of the hidden messages of water and the true power of water amongst others. His experiments have helped us to understand the true power of thought in the 20th century.

One example of this is pivotal. Dr Emoto assembled a number of bottles of water, and labeled them with various words. Things like "Love", "Thank you", "Hate", "You make me sick", and "I will Kill you"

What is particularly note worthy is that the one with "Love" written On was also meditated on by a Buddhist priest, who said prayers over it. What has become important here is that when this bottle was studied under the microscope it was found to have under gone a metamorphosis or change. The water itself had structured itself like a huge flower or snowflake, and was almost brilliant in colour.

By the same token the one that had "hate" written on it had turned into something that looked basically like the inside of a drain. Dark and yellowed, with clear signs of rotting.

What is interesting for me is that the one with "Thank you" On it had also changed for the better and showed a very positive change not unlike its counterpart with Love written on. Thank you. How many times do we say this, or not say this when the case might be. Think about it. When someone turns around to say "Thank you" how does that make you feel? Now, with these experiments we have proved that it's not just our bodies' response to these words that cause this effect. But also there is a physical change that we have a limited understanding of.

One thing worthy of thought is quite unnerving from these results. If our bodies are nearly all water, every time we look in the mirror and criticise ourselves, what do you think we are doing to us? If we can do that to a bottle of water, what are we doing to ourselves, or in fact other people. The case for the existence of karma on the scientific table begins to reveal itself!

We really need to go further into the exploration of the mind in this capacity. Already we are witnessing its abilities which up front appear to converge outside of the brain, but can we measure the strength of these thoughts, and form the basis for the great power of freewill, and its utilisation for the literal creation of good? Does this prove who we are, and maybe also show us a greater understanding of who God really is. After all did he not create us in his own image?

The power of thought can be witnessed in another way even more exciting, and in a way that is totally "Beyond faith"! In other words, this is not about belief, but about facts!

Quantum physics plays an important part. If we study molecules and atoms we witness these quantum particles happily buzzing around. By studying their behavior we become aware of something that is very strange. These particles are not solid, Not matter, Matter does not exist within a quantum wave, that is until observation takes place. As soon as they are "seen" they change from a wave to a particle. It's almost like that old school game of "Peep behind the curtain" where you look at the wall and all your friends have to move towards you. At anytime you turn round and your friends have to freeze. If you see them move their out of the game!

So let me repeat that. These particles do not turn into matter and unless we look at them, which is a staggering thing to have to admit, because everything as far as we are aware is matter. Now, what this could mean in terms of science is that not only does the tree not make a noise when it falls when there is no one to hear it, but it does not exist at all!

Now this is stepping into quantum theory rather than quantum facts. I don't want to muddy the waters too much, so for now I won't explore that. What I will look at with you is how this all proves that not only is there life after death, but that this is part of the communication process that allows mediums to speak to those who, in the words of John Edwards, have crossed over!

The other observation starts to take this onto a level that is more and more starling. These particles are consistently disappearing into nothingness and reappearing as if from nowhere. The burning question then has to be where do they go? They have to be going somewhere? In other words they seem to be able to traverse a dimension, or dimensions that seem at first hand inaccessible to us. This then indicates another realm, another state of existence which you can reimerge from. Again you would be stepping into quantum theory were you to speculate, but the reality is this does indicate another dimension, or world on anti matter? Like a spirit world???

It could just as easily be said that they just go into an alternate reality the same as this, but alternate? In other words just another version of this world. Maybe where there are a whole bunch of scientists wondering where they go when they come back into this world? This if it were the case would prove a multi-dimension existence. However, without trying to seem like I am making it fit, it is arguably more likely that the particle is changing in structure to allow it to do what it does, or it would not vanish at all. This therefore does indicate that the first understanding that it does somehow become etheric in its nature as being more plausible. In other words this just maybe the proof of that after life dimension that we are looking for. There is more evidence to support this outside of the quantum, so that will be later.

Another amazing fact that needs to be explained is that these particles can be photographed in two places at once. Ok lets break this down because it needs to be understood. That is not the same particle being photographed twice. It is not the same particle being photographed in motion, therefore appearing to be in two places at once, this is literally one thing, in two places at the same time. Co-existing in two places at the same time!

Under the laws of known physics this is simply not possible. It cannot happen. Just like the mind or the soul cannot carry on living after the death of the physical body according to many, this cannot happen either, and yet it does!

This concept is of course not new, but has been stated, especially in the east as a known fact for again, thousands of years. I remember, during my time with Patience Denten, when I was learning to understand these spirit links, she told me her guide could be in many places at the same time, and became what she called a universal element, and speak to hundreds of people at the same time in their own languages. Again though this is an observation made of a theory that is based on a dual existence scientific fact of these particles.

Staying with Quantum theory as opposed to quantum fact for the moment, I would just like to offer another hypothesis that is un-validated, but becomes all the more real based on what we have just acknowledged in quantum physics.

We know for a fact that space-time is mutable, that is that we can step outside of time. Einstein proved this. If you were to take a long enough journey into space on your return you would have found that your friends would have aged and you wouldn't or you may meet your great grand children, or that the Earth had been taken over by talking apes, and the statue of liberty was your only clue as to where you were … or maybe not for the last bit!!!, but time will have changed. you will have altered that fabric of your existence.

Based on that understanding, and the behavior of quantum particles, we can assume that assuming you do survive physical death you step outside the space time continuum. So say we have the need to be born, and select a time, a year, like 1926, and we choose that we will pass in 1930, making this a short life, but one that just satisfies what ever need we have.

Maybe again, there is one more thing we need to take from being born into a physical body. Maybe we choose to be born in 1928 to do this. Now we see a problem, we have not actually died yet in the last life! So for two years we must share an existence In other words exist in two places at once. Not possible? Tell that to these particles!

What we now need to ask ourselves is whether this proves that we are in actual fact all at some level the same person, but at various levels of existence. It would seem likely if we change our concept of what mankind really is. This does not mean we all merge into one lump of playdough in the afterlife. Being able to channel we know that's not the case, but what it might just do is give us a new idea behind the meaning of the brotherhood of man, and certainly explain once and for all the true understanding of the eastern concept of Karma, and therefore, what we do to others we really are doing to ourselves at some point!!!

One thing as a medium I can confirm is that we don't automatically have the answers when we pass into the spirit world. In fact there is far little change than you realise. We are a long way from knowing for sure, and death does not bring the answers.

But back into quantum physics rather than quantum theory, this validates life after death because, as I said earlier, the particles do not become waves until they are observed. Now, this observer. (a word which the scientists would rather use as oppose to spirit or soul, I suppose its diplomatic, you might just upset less people that way), Is NOT in the brain. They have looked at every part of the brain and it simply is NOT there.

There is no reason to think that the observer stops observing at the point of death because it does not rely on the physical body. It carries on doing what it always does, creating matter!

This also lead us to another amazing fact that, if you understood the impact of what I have said, you must have taken on board that we are all creators in our own right. Creating a collective world in a collective consciousness, so yes we are all God, and thus provably created in his own image!

One thing this revelation did was make me think about my own faith. In the Bible, faith is obviously a huge discussion point, and Jesus even goes to say that if we really believe it enough, and had enough faith, we could move a mountain. Many scholars have of course seen this as another metaphor, but when you take into account what we now know to be true, then this really is the case, which leads to a question that I don't even want to try and answer yet. Did Christ have an understanding of quantum physics? If so that would certainly explain many sayings that have been reported through biblical text. It would even explain his abilities because once you have understood the concept, in theory you should be able to effect the quantum field, change it, will things to happen in your day, and at some stage they will!

I sometimes try and do this where possible. Sometimes I am not able to achieve this, sometimes I am shocked by the results. Though its not won me the lottery. I have looked for proof of this though. One example was that I willed myself to come into contact with exactly £2.49 .I selected that as an odd amount to reduce the possibility of coincidence. Then I asked that it be brought into play to prove that my mind is in charge of the reality.

Without a lie that night I stepped out to walk the dogs, and on the floor was exactly that in change that someone had dropped. £2.49. Of course I tried it again the next night but it didn't happen.

The moral if anything though comes from Dr Emoto and the water experiments. Just remember we are 97% water ourselves, so what are we really doing to ourselves?

CHAPTER THREE

"Orbs and light anomalies –
Separating the facts and fiction"

I WAS WATCHING a TV programme called Spook school. In it they got a whole bunch of people together to basically teach them how to explore the paranormal, and go on Ghosthunts of their own, using a wide range of electrical equipment, which is available to anyone wishing to purchase it.

I will not go into great detail with my opinion, but did not feel confident at the expertise being related in this programme regarding this subject matter,

In Parapsychology every door has to be covered. Before coming to specific conclusions on anything, especially what may and may not have a paranormal nature.

The team in question debunked orbs as dust particles, Orbs being the strange discs of light that seem to be turning up on peoples photographs all over the world right now.

By wearing marigolds and sprinkling dust down in front of a camera lens they were able to photograph the dust, which appeared as round coloured discs of light. They then announced that they had debunked orbs, and also suggested that the reason we pick dust up now is that digital cameras have the flash too near the lens.

In fact there are numerous cases of orbs being seen on standard 35mm pictures, and in fact its only now that people looking over their old photographs are only now recognising them for what they are. Jane Goldman, the TV presenter looked into this, and consulted a photograph expert in this field, who in fact having studied this himself, found no plausible link to orbs and anything natural. In his words he was "open minded".

Regardless of whether or not orbs are spiritual emanations, or have a natural explanation, a true parapsychologist would view both sides with equal measure, taking into consideration that people who claim orbs are sprit, also claim that they appear where there is a spiritual meeting, or when talked about. So for this reason the experiment can't be conclusive because it should have been done only in a time and place that is distant from any meeting or discussion relating to the paranormal. A school of paranormal activity is therefore inappropriate!

The fact remains that in all likelihood they got pictures of dust that day, but they will not know for sure unless experiments are done under proper conditions. Such experiments have been conducted.

July 21st 2007, the daily mail published an article with the heading *" **Is this the proof spirits do exist**"* It followed Professor Klaus Heinemann's discovery of small light discs around a gathering of spiritual healers in photographs.

Professor Heinemann, like anyone would make the assumption that these discs of light were all due to known phenomena, i.e. flash anomalies, water particles or dust etc…

Heinemann then conducted a rigorous exploration of the phenomena. As a NASA scientist no detail was left uncovered, and he deployed all of his expertise, which included examining matter down to atomic levels of optical resolution.

Heinemann and his wife then started taking hundreds of pictures at random in as many ways possible. It was difficult for him as a scientist with a reputation to uphold, but in the end he had to concede that these pictures could be repeated….but only if you ask!!!

Now this is true, and you can do this yourself with a little time and patience. By asking they will appear with you for the camera, and also leave you alone if you ask them to. He rapidly concluded that you didn't have to speak. The entities seemed to respond just as well to your thoughts. I have done this myself in a series of pictures, asking "Orbs" to appear, and then asking them to leave. The sequence of pictures of me doing this clearly demonstrates this.

As a scientist, who also happens to be a keen photographer it was easy for Heinemann to eliminate dust particles as being the probable cause, despite the fact that these "Natural" orbs can look identical, they have a notable difference that has been now studied under laboratory conditions. This is a fact, not fiction, and anyone who continues to state that ALL orbs are the result of natural occurrences is either in denial or a member of "The earth is really flat" Conspiracy theorists.

Heinemann set up dozens of experiments often involving more than one camera at a time. One of the first things that he established was that the orbs are fast! Very fast, and recorded speed in excess of 500 miles per hour. Now this is recorded speed intimating that they may be capable of a lot more.

Heinemann also found that during his experiments of two or more cameras, when he used twin cameras to capture an anomaly from two different angles, a single orb would appear but only in one of the two images taken simultaneously, which proved that the orb was actively making itself known to a camera deliberately and by design, making a choice of who, or what camera it was going to show itself to, if at all.

As a result of the test so far. Heinemann was forced kicking and screaming to the conclusion that he was witnessing something of intelligence, and consequently something paranormal.

Heinemann made the following statement to the daily mail in the July of 2007:

> "There is no doubt in my mind that orbs maybe one of the most significant 'outside of this reality' phenomena mankind has ever witnessed. Until now there has been a huge amount of anecdotal evidence that the spirit world exists. Thanks to digital photography we can see it for the first time. We are dealing with a non physical all be it real phenomena"

There are a growing number of scientists who work in this field who themselves offer validation to this. Especially Miceal Ledwith of the University of Ireland who co-wrote the breakthrough book "The orb project" with Heinemann, along side William Tiller.

That same year there was a conference in Arizona where a number of scientists backed up Karl, and Miceal's research. Their conclusions, which seemed so far reaching now, can be viewed with the opinion that this might just be the start of the new way we view the universe.

This opinion was pioneered by scientists Peter Fenwick who claimed not that long ago that life after death would soon have to be taught in schools as a fact!

Professor William Tiller, a theoretical physicist who spent 35 years researching consciousness, and matter at Sanford university in California reminded everyone at the conference that…

> "What we see with our eyes is less than 10% of the known universe. This is because human vision can only operate with a limited range of the electromagnetic spectrum. For instance we cannot see radio waves which carry huge amounts of information, yet we know they exist".

By a similar token, Miceal Ledwith, a former professor of theology who for ten years was president of Maynooth college at the National university of Ireland reminded skeptics that in 1861 Dr Ignaz Semmelweis had claimed that there might be some unseen link between surgeons who didn't wash their hands, and the high rate of infection in child birth. His mainstream colleagues ridiculed him, and yet he had found evidence of what is now commonly known as Bacteria.

Ledwith went on to say…

> "In my mind there is no doubt that the orb phenomena is real, and deserved to be taken seriously"

Ledwith, a member of the theological commission at the Vatican has a collection of orb pictures, which now number 100.000

"They come in all sizes ranging from a few inches to several feet across, sometimes they appear alone, and other times hundreds appear in all colours from white to blue, green, rose and even gold. Over time I realised that a flash seemed essential to capture them, even in daylight, this is because we can only see orbs through the process in physics known as FLUORESCENCE. The camera flash sparks fluorescence making them visible to the camera"

I believe that they might be the spirits of those who have passed on, or some spiritual teachers, or spirits waiting to be born or reborn into physical bodies, from nature spirits to spirits of just pure energy that have never been incarnated into physical form"

Many of the scientists at the conference believe that orbs are plasma, like balls of energy, but an energy that can be detected by physical means, which appears to have a sense of control over its shape and form. It is true to say that they are mostly photographed at spiritual gatherings or where interest is shown in them or anything paranormal. Hence my criticism of spook schools attempts to debunk them as dust during the spook school. In fact they are witnessed so much around healing sessions that it is now accepted that they play a part in the healing process.

Moving on from the scientists, it has to be said that there are a number of things going on here. Clearly orbs respond to your mind, or thoughts, so clearly they can react to your desires or your wishes. Again I refer to my series of pictures where I ask Orbs to appear, then ask them to leave just by thinking it.

Now with a strong scientific basis for this, I have a question to ask you. If orbs can absorb our thoughts and hear them, is it not likely that they can communicate back having looked at the evidence presented so far? If your answer is yes then this is proof on the scientific table of what we call mediumship. If your answer is no, then would you kindly go back to the beginning of this chapter, and start again.

If you get to this stage a second time and still your answer is no, then please don't continue. Just pop this book into the next boot sale or even the bin!

The spirits energy is the orb, not the spirit itself. A bit like a torch representing the spirit, but the light it produces the orb. The torch of course can point that light anywhere, and of course change its appearance by placing something in front of the beam for example.

The spirit enters our aura, and feeds us information through the temporal lobe area of the brain, therefore side stepping our own thoughts and feelings from the mind, but controlling every function from sight, hearing, seeing, feeling and smelling. These facilities are now under their control, just like a new DVD in a recorder. The recorder works the same no matter what DVD is in it. This is why you will hear a medium saying " I smell smoke, I feel anger, I see a gun etc.

The amount of information that is passed on can vary, and some people are better side steppers than others, hence the appearance of good and bad mediumship, and some that might appear to be better than others.

I will explain about these spirit intelligence's in greater detail later, and talk about their natural environment etc, for the moment what is important is the acceptance of what is going on here.

What is important is that we have established spirit communication, which to a degree is now "Beyond Faith" When it comes to personal pictures Kim and I have a collection of original pictures that are of various types of orbs and manifestations.

There seems to be a pattern for people wishing to take pictures of orbs. Like mediumship development nothing at first, then with time and patience, asking them to come. One or two light anomalies make themselves known, then more. Its as if the energy needs to build itself up, then all of a sudden you have a room full of orbs revealing themselves at will.

Now interestingly in the book "Beyond photography" by Katie Price and John Pickering, the authors went on to start to get other things happen after a while. It was like a specific sequence of events. After a period of time Katie started to get like explosions of light that really in all honesty looked like Katie had photographed a moth, what looked like wings being clearly visible.

But what is strange is that this image kept happening again and again, so if it were a moth, why does it suddenly become repetitive? Their conclusion therefore has to be that it's not. It's as if the photographic effort that we have put in now seems to be rewarded with a further development.

Next comes an even further development when we witness swirls of mist and plasma emanations (not unlike what was once known as ectoplasm, a word we seem to want to distance ourselves from as it became synonymous with Edwardian fake pictures).

The best thing is that the plasma itself will evolve into manifestations very often recognised as loved ones, friends that we would actually recognise.

(see "Tatiana" at the end of the book).

I know these events as they progress are general to everyone because they occurred to us in the same sequence and time movements as they did to Katie in her book, beyond photography, First orbs, then the "Moths" as it were though of course they are not. Then the plasma mists and full apparitions.

I should not keep knocking Spook school, but I should mention that they were shown pictures similar to this "Stage two" of events. The lady who showed them had wondered if they were some sort of angelic manifestation. Having, or appearing to have little knowledge of the exploration of orb phenomena they instantly dismissed them as just insects caught in the flash.

My interpretation, based on the events in beyond photography and my own, indicate that she may have been correct in her assumption. Enough said on that.

One thing to be aware of is that orbs can be seen on cameras due to the sensitivity to the opposite ends of the spectrum I.e. Infa red and ultra violet

Now, people around the world who have no knowledge of this have been complaining to camera manufacturers, that their cameras are being ruined by " Light balls or bubbles" so camera manufacturers have been tying to desensitize cameras to this phenomena by building into the cameras a series of what are known as hot mirrors, which will stop orbs from showing themselves!

So if you want to take pictures of orbs, or buy a camera that will do the job, you have to take your sky TV remote to the camera shop, and activate it through the lens. If you can see the light, then the camera will work fine. If not then you need to try another camera till you find one that's suitable. Alternatively you can buy a Sony camera which has a night shot mode. By activating this hot mirror is moved aside. Never attempt to remove the hot mirror from a camera yourself.

* Never try to take orb pictures in a rural or dusty environment
* To find a real orb, look to see if there is an object between the orb and the camera. Water droplets and dust particles must be within a few feet of the lens
* Look for an orb in rapid motion. See if it has a tail
* Look to see if in a series of pictures one shows orbs and the other doesn't

Look to see if the same orbs are shown in successive image frames.

CHAPTER FOUR

"Living in a spirit world"

IT IS IMPOSSIBLE when it comes to great mediums not to mention the name of Steve Holbrook. He is up there with Keith Charles, Gordon Smith, T J Higgs, The only reason though that I have singled Steve out for the moment is because of an incident that happened to him which is a perfect example what I wish to approach in this chapter.

I have said all along that I don't want anything in here that is not to some capacity or validated by science, but hope that you will bare with me while I relate the following event.

Steve related this in his book "Light in the darkness" Which was written by my good friend James Christie, who also published it. This story is of how Steve was awoken in the early hours of the morning by the phone ringing. A friend of his was calling and appeared to be in a bit of a state.

The person on the other end of the phone claimed that for the duration of that night they had been suffering from an "Apparition" or "Ghost" that had apparently just 'appeared' from the fireplace. They went on to report that this ghost was quite solid, and wearing what they described as old-fashioned clothes. They were clearly upset, and hoped that Steve being a medium and clairvoyant would be able to come and sort this out. Now Steve is no ones fool. He has been on TV, been wrote about, spoke about, and attracted big audiences, in the past up to 800 have queued up to see him demonstrate.

Eventually after a second call validating what was going on he threw his jeans on and in the early hours of the morning drove around to the friends home.

Steve was skeptical that anything would happen. It all seemed quite far fetched, and Can tell you that in this work you do get a lot of calls from a lot of cranks or people who believe themselves into an event if that makes sense.

After a period of waiting, and growing impatient, suddenly before his eyes appeared a small man in front of him, as if from no where! A solid figure wearing exactly what his friends had described.

Steve by his own admittance was scared. He had not experienced this phenomenon before so why would he not be? The apparition appeared to be aware of the people in the room, and its eyes fixed on Steve!

Then, without warning it reached over and grabbed his leg. Steve felt its touch and let out a bit more than a whimper!

The apparition eventually vanished as mysteriously as it had arrived. What Steve said after is the interesting part, and offers the reason why I wanted to relate this to you? He said it wasn't at all like when he channels spirit on the platform. When they connect to him there is this beautiful feeling of love and light, Sheer joy. I, like many others, have seen Steve reduced to tears during such a session at the passion he feels during such moments.

Now this was not like that. It was uncomfortable, a little scary, unpredictable, and certainly not enjoyable.

So what we are dealing with in this scenario is a spirit energy that in many ways does not seem to relate to energy that is communicated through the church or platform, and consequently through our auras, the temporal lobe, and the mind. But instead appeared extraneously in our environment…type A!

This is why when I investigated a haunting, for want of a better word; my approach is entirely different to my work as a medium. I appreciate that you can contact the "other" types of energy in the same way. " Most haunted" would have us believe it so, but I would rather approach this other form of spirit visitation from a different angle.

I was called out to Newhaven, about one and half-hours from where I live. The girl whom I went to see I shall refer to as Lydia, had been toubled by a similar type of spirit manifestation, and was very concerned as now it was starting to effect her two children. Her son who was about 6 or 7 years old, and her daughter about 3.

Lydia was no longer living with the children's father, so she was by an large dealing with this alone, though her Mum and sister were very good. The children, especially the boy were being disturbed nightly by what they described as a frightening old man who was standing by the side of the bed.

The boy was at times too terrified to go upstairs, and the situation was starting to get out of control. She had not taken the incident to be paranormal at first, but viewed it as being just night terrors children sometimes get, that is until it started to also target her.

She had just gone to bed, and had not been asleep long when she woke up to the feeling of being unable to breathe. She clearly felt as if her throat was being squeezed… Panicking, assuming someone had broken in she kicked out expecting her foot to come into contact with a human torso, but it just thrust into thin air. Then suddenly the feeling stopped just as quickly as it had started.

Choking, Lydia managed to switch the light on. There was of course no one there, so she put it down to a bad dream that "seemed too real"!

In the morning, after a restless night, she caught sight of herself in the mirror. Around her neck and throat there were finger marks. This was when she contacted me! The following Sunday the children were dispatched to their Dads and I arrived about 3pm. I was met by Lydia, her Mum, and her sister (who was known to me as she had been sitting in a development circle).

I didn't have the electrical equipment that I use now to gather evidence for this, so just relied on what I called my tuning in ability as it were.

I must have been trying for an hour and made no connections with the house at all, the only links I got were family members.

In the end I must confess that I felt that there must be nothing going on at the house at all, and had decided to leave. Lydia was mortified, as she had placed so much expectancy on me, so I agreed to one last look round.

To this day I can only guess as to why I didn't find this connection when I first went there, but this time it was different. As I went upstairs, in a sort of clairvoyant glaze I saw a man standing outside the child's bedroom this was not an apparition, so it was as if I were looking at a type B spirit communication. I knew that he could manifest in the same ways Steve's "Friend" had, otherwise he would not have left those marks on Lydia's neck, the main difference was that this one was apparently hostile.

I tried to send my thoughts out to him to let him know that if he wanted to communicate, I would listen! At this point I remember I sort of stepped back, and took a side ways look down the landing, there was a lady on the stairs, lying as I turned, with her neck cocked awkwardly to one side and her arms out stretched. Almost as if in a gesture of "help me"

A little shaken I looked back inside the room, and saw the man standing there in shirtsleeves, dark trousers and braces. That was about all I could make out clearly. Then I became aware of the house changing around me. The bathroom changed from a modern suit to a single sink unit, and the layout was different, though I could honestly not take on board how.

Then in a vision I saw him and the lady. He seemed to be shouting but I heard nothing but silence, and she was distressed. In a horrifying moment I saw him throw her down the stairs. I knew instantly that he had broken her neck. This must of course have been how she died.

This must have been the horrifying event that this poor little boy witnessed night after night. I decide to try and speak to both of these entities as they had both in some capacity made themselves known to me I would rather communicate than jump straight into a traditional cleansing where possible.

I decide to work from the bedroom, and get Liz, Lydia's sister to help me, having had some experience in this area. We sat on the floor, on our knees, facing each other and sent out a prayer. We both felt that we had drawn his attention. The room went icy cold, and we both started to feel anxious. All at once I started to hear what I can only describe as a muffled voice, sometimes from inside my head, sometimes from the outside. I asked him to identify himself to us.

In front of my eyes for the second time the environment changed. A side -ways glance into the landing, I saw the room revert to how I'd seen it before. Particularly noticeable was the hallway leading to the bathroom.

In my mind I wandered to the end of the hall, and again I could hear shouting and screaming, and once more that earlier image flashed in front of my eyes. I'll be honest, I didn't know what to do next for the moment. Was I seeing this because it was residual, that is ingrained on the atmosphere, was it because I could link to the lady, or was it the man reaching out, trying to find some peace in his heart. This is the problem with mediumship. Sometimes you don't know how you're getting it or why you're getting it. You just know your getting it, and until I was certain I would not be able to move with this.

Again I prayed, harder than I ever had in my life. It was as if I became "aware" … I knew for example that this had been a man of faith despite his actions. Then I felt his anger. I also became "aware" that his rages were the result of mental illness on the earth plane, and it was then I felt his guilt.

There was no excuse for what he had done to Lydia. But in a way I could not help but feel compassion to this type of entity, (type A), because in this case, the entity refused to pass into the domain that would allow him to shed just one more body, and go home to that natural state we sometimes like to call heaven.

As a catholic in life, I now understood. He thought that if he went through the light he would be persecuted and go to hell for what he had done. He could see no other way out other than to hide?

This highlights what I have always said that we die twice. Rather like an egg, the main part of death comes from cracking that shell, but there is another layer of skin which also needs to come off, a process of elevation on a mental level.

The spirit body in essence is a strong Electro-magnetic energy field with mind and soul intact. An energy body that can be sensed felt and measured.

This energy is "near" to our own level of existence, or so is clearly perceived or picked up, so in effect we have a haunting. To right the balance here, all I do was during this mind link, open up a huge vortex, like a huge ball of light. I kept telling him "No one will judge you, no one will judge you, God is love, and tried to encourage him towards this vortex.

It took over an hour and a half, then what I saw not only astonished me, but will remain with me the rest of my life.

The light opened up to engulf the room, and the lady, whose image I had clearly seen on the stairs stepped from inside of it. Clearly she had never been earth bound and had come in visitation to maybe watch over him, protect the kids, or try and persuade him that it was ok to join her and that he would not go to hell.

I saw her touch his shoulder in my mind and as she did so the light disappeared and them with it! She had somehow used the power that Liz and I had produced, knowing why we were there into making one final effort, and they were gone!

Liz and I were exhausted. It was like everything we had was drained from us. We even had trouble standing up. Than I heard a voice. This time it was from that place where I hear spirit from platform. The voice said simply "Thank you"

I could not tell you for sure if it was him or her as they all sound the same to me, male and female, but I would love to think that it was him.

The next day I waited with great anticipation for the follow up call. The news was good. The boy had come home from his Dads, and was very nervous about being sent upstairs for his bath with the words that every child his age has to endure from their Mum on a Sunday night "Come on, have your bath you got school tomorrow" (yeah thanks Mum).

He had hesitated on the stairs but when he eventually went up, Lydia was paralysed by the screaming and the commotion, She ran up there as fast as she could go

" Mum he's gone, he's gone" the boy shouted. The burning question is, how did he know so quickly? That's one I can't answer.

The other question is why is it that the entity and his wife retained a likeness to their physical bodies? The hypothesis again comes from the basis of quantum physics, and extends also to why when passing into that second stage of exist i.e., the spirit form or world, does it appear to retain the characteristics of this world. I.e. recognizable trees, animals, buildings, shrubs, and even domains.

The answer is apparent from the earlier scientific exploration of the quantum hypothesis. Its because up until that time, it is the only way we know how to existance! If we created this reality, created this matter via observation, and we did this outside of the physical body, (which we now know because that's where we assume the "Observer" to be), then, there is no justifiable reason for that to change just because the physical body dies. The process of creating remains the same regardless.

Also this environment, part of the memory is recognisable to us, and therefore comfortable. Without the birth process, one would really have to question as to whether we would know how to exist. Would it be just like one great white canvass but with no point, and coloured in by the process of creation?

This process indicates that we are all creators, all apart of a shared creation process, like a dream but shared? All those different levels of us coming together to form matter regardless of which side of life we are, or whether we have a physical body.

As for that old man, he was not being judged, nether would he have been, he was simply judging himself!

To lighten the load a bit, Here's a funny story about sex.

I was reading a book by medium Sylvia Brown on the after life. This was quite a few years ago now, and was horrified at a statement she made. Basically that "Sex in the afterlife was better than here and your orgasm thousands of times more powerful"

Needless to say I was mortified at this statement. For me the spirit world was a domain of sanctity and had to be taken seriously, and I felt at the time that she was undermining everything that I had stood for.

So, challenging this because to me sex was of course a physical thing on the earth used just for the reproductive process, I started to write her a letter.

It was a crazy notion because the chances of her reading the letter or even acknowledging it were ridiculously unlikely.

As I set about my protest, my guide drew close to me, and I could feel that all-powerful feeling of comfort that I get in his presence. I heard him very clearly question my motive, and in no uncertain terms I voiced my opinion of Sylvia Browns notions.

He then asked me what the nearest state of existence was to being in the world of spirit without actually passing over. I must confess that as I heard the question clearly, there was no room for doubt, it was there, but actually I didn't really understand it.

I went through all the possibilities from out of body experiences to near death experiences, but nothing seemed to fit.

Then I thought "Dreams", the dream state? it was almost like it all fell into place, and those familiar, guiding me then saying "Have you ever had an erotic dream?". I searched my mind for that one "Kylie Minogue" moment, and realised that the point was I had created a reality in my dream, or by having the dream. And in that we all wore clothes went to the library the Theatre, and the spirit world is part of that process, so yes in fact the plausibility of sharing sexual content with someone you love is not out of the realms of possibility after all. I did not send my letter.

Some people say guides are just our own consciousness, some like myself, choose to regard then as separate energies, as much as we are separate from other people in life. I think based on what we have learned its safe to say a combination of both. Many orthodox Christians say that guides are demons!! If you take anything from this book it would be the understanding that if guides were demons then quantum physics proves you have created that yourself!

So anyway we can now safely state that there is a spiritual domain, a place to go, a heaven if you like, and what lies beyond that is as open to speculation as anything. This world exists and in it we can travel anywhere just by thinking it, we can hear each other just by knowing, also hear information in large numbers of people at a time and don't have to worry about a language barrier.

This is why mediumship can be difficult, as this process becomes part of that manner of communication to people. That said to, sometimes I get all this information crammed into my head at once, and before I can pass it on I literally have to dissect and interpret It bit by bit, unfortunately that does and can lead to errors.

During his experiments with spirit a man called William Stanton Moses asked a spirit energy to locate a book in a library, then locate a certain page in that book, and read a paragraph whilst dictating it through the gift of automatic writing. It was instant, the writing coming through the medium that did no more than hold the pen over the paper. When the book was eventually located and the page found it was found to be correct. What had been instant to spirit took them a good half-hour to do.

A lady whom I shall call Sylvia came to me for a reading a long time ago. She had lost her daughter. Although evidence came through, you could tell it was never going to be enough for her.

When you're grieving nothing a medium does can ever be enough, but people have such expectancies.

At the end of the session she asked me if her child missed her. I clearly heard the word "No" straight back at me.

I was of course very diplomatic, and tried to explain that not only was her child always with her, but because spirit step outside of our time, the feeling the child would have is more like being left for five minutes while Mum pops to the shops, and not this sense of separation, that pain is ours.

We always stay linked. I liken it to the person who has died, just being in the kitchen while you are in the living room, but if they were in the kitchen you could still shout and tell them what's on the TV, and they would know. They could still hear you, and therefore still be apart of what's going on, and still have an opinion on it.

I believe that the spirit world does sub-divide into various levels. However, I can't prove it, so I will not go deeply into that, Needless to say there are good and sound reasons why I have arrived at that conclusion For many years spiritual people have classed spirit on the other side as "Vibrations". The way this is understood is that as an energy source, we omit just that, a kind of frequency, theirs being quite high next to ours on the earth plane. The happier you are the higher your vibration.

In order to link with us the spirit has to reduce that frequency to something that is closely compatible to ours.

This is why we link to type A energies easier because there vibration is that much lower, and therefore closer to our own.

Many times I have heard how people say that they don't feel connected to their loved ones in spirit. Usually when they are sad and grieving, the processes that allow communication means that spirit have to lower their vibration to get the link. If we are really down in a state of depression our own vibration will dip accordingly rendering it very difficult for spirit to make themselves known. It's a bit like trying to breathe through mud for them!

I have a great illustration of the difference between the physical and spiritual world. Non UK readers will just have to bare with me for the moment, but there was in the 70's a TV add for Cadburys flake. A girl would be painting a picture of trees, and then suddenly it rained on the picture. After her chocolate to cheer her up she noticed that the rain on the picture had blended the trees all into one, and it looked better.

The point is that this is a great representation of both worlds. This side of life being represented by the first picture. The trees are all solid and individual, but the second the rain hits, and they all blend into one we can see how all of that picture merges into one, and the trees become part of each other.

CHAPTER FIVE

"Manifestations"

ENERGY CAN'T be destroyed. Einstein proved that and the very laws of nature suggests that.

We are all surrounded by the electrical energies that follow the contours of the body. That means that this energy will be an exact representation of you, and look just like you! Mediums and spiritual people spoke a very long time ago about the existence of the astral body long before it was proven when "Semyon Davidovitch Krirlian" took the first picture of it.

What was curious was that after developing the Kirlian camera, he observed that it was not just people, but anything living that had this extra electrical body linked to its living counterpart.

Taking the first picture of this kind of a leaf he noticed the aura, but what was more curious was that when he snipped a piece of the leaf off in the corner, the aura remained unchanged. In other words could not be damaged.

This in itself is remarkable evidence that when we die, we are not necessarily restored, but never lost that part of us in the first place, so in other words an amputee would always retain a connection to the lost limb.

The only reason a medium might not see that restored appendix is that the message giver may well be trying to convey the essence of who he was if a name wasn't assessable.

That said, because we have proved that your mind is in control of a situation, and that manipulation of the physical, I remember an incident where a group of mediums were called out to a haunting. The presence was of a young boy, In life he had sadly been a hunchback, who had been continually bullied.

When he was seen by the mediums, he was as he was in life, with the hunch back, as he was passed "Into the light", I.e. going from type A to type B, he had left his deformity behind, and came back perfect.

The whole universe is made up of electrons Protons and neutrons pulsating with electrical charges. Now these charges produce E.M.F's. Electro magnetic fields.

This is a highly crucial piece of information because when it comes to detecting the presence of a spirit, we can confirm this presence by picking up its E.M.F". Of late experienced researchers into the paranormal have found that spirit can use their natural E.M.F discharge as a means of communication.

Put simply, an E.M.F detector can literally locate the presence of a spirit. The electrical field it measured is what we call milligauss. The higher the reading the greater the electrical strength. If this reading goes off the scale we have made detection.

A sprit can move that energy towards the detector by design allowing it to register. This then can become a sort of electrical communication board deploying the method of one strike for yes and two for no!

I use a number of different E.M.F detectors. There is a commonly used tri field detector, which originally was pretty much the only one you could get. Then variations were produced, my favorite being the one used on ghosthunters, and the one I used when I was involved in a TV programme called "Bryonny makes a zombie movie", but the less said about that the better.

This meter is called simply the K2, and can easily be found on e-bay. Remarkably inexpensive it is a colour coded E.M.F with light display going from green to amber to red. Green is ok, amber detects a presence, but red is the ultimate aim.

What you have to be aware of is that there are a number of natural sources of E.M.F s which have to be eliminated before you establish whether you are picking up E.M.F s from spirit or a natural source, like a junction box or something.

So before you investigate a haunting, you need to sweep the area with your K2, just to establish where there might be hidden cables or generators which might wrong foot you.

In a similar capacity Spirit emanations also produce free floating electrical particles called Ions. So by the same token we can also use an Ion detector, which should be self explanatory.

Now, all these natural energy sources are found around the presence of orb phenomena, and so very often an Orb presence will be found during the exhibition of E.M.Fs or ions. This is why I think that it's important to keep taking pictures. My only criticism of ghosthunters is that this isn't done enough.

If you can afford to spend nearly two grand on a thermal imaging camera, then good, but for most of us digital pictures are all we got!

Nothing winds me up more that a bunch of surly self proclaimed paranormal investigators that do nothing more than wander around all night, then sit down with an upturned glass and a bunch of alphebettie spaghetti letters! This is not gathering evidence. Many might argue that doing a ouija board is gathering evidence. Well maybe it is to some degree but it is not conclusive, and can be dangerous if not done correctly. It's a bit like living in one of the worst trouble spots you can picture, and opening your front door and saying "Everyone in"!!

The first person to walk through that door might tell you that they are Dr Jones from Acacia Avenue, but it does not mean that they are!

That's said I would permit the use of a board if there is absolutely no doubt as to the authenticity of the communicator.

So when we take pictures, hopefully we will get enough to either recognise faces, or even better, our actual loved ones. I am fortunate enough to have found such evidence, as you will see in the pictures.

So what are we seeing?

Well, after Orbs bunch together, they tend to be able to utalise energy especially human energy like Ki or Chi

As I said before spirit need this natural energy to manifest, whether it be this Chi or Ki, or a network of underground cables (Like in the case of the Eastbourne waterworks investigation) or a power grid, or quite simply people who have a natural abundance of this energy.

I did Aikido for eleven years and learned a lot about the development and harnessing of Ki, which I learned to describe as a natural human fluid that manifests from the solar plexus. We all have this to varying degrees and the capability to developing it. Not wanting to demean its existence, but its easily comparable to say the force from star wars, and like wise can be directed by thought outside of the physical body, which of course quantum physics now shows us.

So this energy source can also be tapped into by spirit manifestations, hence "Poltergeist" cases, where objects can be seen to be thrown around. This can only be done with this "Fuel source" so historically the best way to tackle a situation like this is to find the source and cut it off! End of problem

This is why there have been a great deal of poltergeist cases centered around a young females entering the throws of adolescence. The emotional link between this and the generation of Ki has long time been understood.

This is a good point because again it shows how this energy is controlled by a mind, or an emotional state, and therefore can occur uncontrolled as in the movie Carrie.

This is why Shaolin priests and martial artists have abilities to punch through walls, and evidently stand on the sharp end of a spear without it causing so much as splinter of blood.

So it is self evident that the more of this energy we carry, the stronger spirit are when they work with us, not just in physical mediumship (where evidence is obtained outside of the consciousness), but mental mediumship to People who develop or have developed a strong attachment to this natural energy are usually able to hear better and give more concise messages.

Chi, Ki is linked to breath, the life force! Its development is rather simplistic, and simply involves breathing exercises where you would say inhale for seven seconds, hold your breath for seven seconds, and breath out for say twelve seconds. When exhaling your focus should be on your center, your "Hara" which is two inches below your belly button! Forget the diaphragm.

In your mind you need to picture that energy extending outwards. In martial arts we do a test called ""the unbendable arm" Where you send that energy down your arm and totally relax the muscles. If this works then no matter what, no one can bend or even move your arm.

I have personally witnessed extensions of this process where a small Japanese man placed his big toe over a staff, and no one could move it. Not the toe or the staff! He then proceeded to sit on his knees and remained there by sheer will power alone while six burly men tried to lift him off the ground and failed.

A man called just "Kormar" back in the seventies was driven over by a bulldozer and was unhurt, as well as being sandwiched in a bed of nails which he got a dozen men to also sit on.

So potentially this energy is very powerful, so when "borrowed" by a spirit visitor it can be devastating. Hence the Enfield poltergeist case, again a haunting in the seventies that had huge media coverage due to its velocity.

Personally, one way I would have tried to deal with this is to remove the energy source which in this case was one of the daughters, and teach her how to "drain" this energy away so that you have depleted the fuel, stopping the car from working!

Now in the olden days (An expression I made up when I was six, just thought I would share it with you) This manifested from the medium and was recognised and known as "Human fluid", but, when mixed with natural bodily components, and combined with the atmosphere it was known as "Ectoplasm". In this state it was visible, and mutable.

Ectoplasm is a very unpopular word today because it brings to mind all those awful post Victorian pictures of fake ectoplasm, which by today's standards can be seen for what they are. In reality mediums were condemned and criticized, and had "Witchfinders" invade sittings and throw on the lights to try and expose the trickery! This of course is very detrimental to the medium and can make them ill or even kill them!

Exposing the frauds is also of course big business to this day and I have already covered that, but The concept of using what is only in the "Physical body" i.e. the brain and known mind to explain something that occurs outside of this is simply not realistic.

This is why the "Cold reading" Explanation for what we do is not viable. Cold reading is the name given to an attempt to dupe someone by asking questions, studying body movement, the clever use of words etc. As quantum physics shows us what we do is outside of that control, outside of the field of psychology, and so cannot be measured in that way. So in principle if someone has a reading, then goes, and something is said, even by a known fraud, we need to explore whether that was right simply because it was part of the quantum field. In other words, we were supposed to hear it!

We have also seen than science validates the fact that spirit are everywhere, and can respond to our thoughts. Contact seems to be made via the temporal lobe of the brain, rendering our bodies nothing more than elaborate DVD players.

Therefore we have to conclude that despite there being good and bad examples of mediumship, the sheer will-power of wanting to be a medium makes it so, providing it is done with honesty and sincerity, because spirit influence our thoughts and minds once we have given permission. Bad interpretation or a less than adequate DVD player (Brain and body) is more likely the reason behind poor quality mediumship.

It only becomes cold reading when there is a deliberate attempt to fraud a reading for gain. Spirit will not work with you under those circumstances. Some people are NOT a natural doorway for spirit even though they want it badly. This is sad, and very often these people refuse to accept that maybe this time round it's just not meant to be.

Many parapsychologists seem to be either against or for what we do. Not many seem to sit on the fence. They are supposed to be unbiased but the ones I have studied are anything but, specially one whose work I studied while doing my parapsychology course, strongly giving the impression that no matter what was said he would go the opposite.

So a parapsychologist seems to start an investigation either as a believer or a non -believer and either way this does seem to effect their conclusions when dealing with the paranormal.

The exception is Ceiron o'Keefe. Although I haven't met him I hold him in the highest regard as far as being fair minded and open to possibilities. As I have already said this is important. Close the mind they go!

My wife's brother John John. (This is not a typing error, he is known as John John rather than John because his Dad is also called John) !!!!

I often wonder if John had a son would we have to call him John John John...?

Anyway that aside, John John, who at the time was extremely skeptical, came round about two months after Kim and I had bought our first monitor, and with great enthusiasm Kim wanted to show her brother the Orbs.

Everything was set up, which was our original monitor, which unfortunately "Blew up" the night of the ocean bowling investigation, more on that later-

.... And we were greeted by a beautiful display of orbs! Dancing around all Four Corners of the room. John John was not impressed and denounced the activity as nothing more than dust.

He then took a couple of cushions and banged them together in front of the camera creating a snow storm of dust that was more visible and just as spectacular as the orbs.

" See its just dust" he said, and I could see on Kim's face that he had sold her the concept of perhaps she had been duped.

This may well have been the case but for one thing. From that night on for the next two months when we set the monitor up nothing happened! Not one single light anomaly.We could make dust, but that was definitely not what we had seen.

There was no voluntary light display., in other words they were either sulking, or more likely trying to show us that they were not there to demonstrate the fact they had been if that makes sense.

Then, as suddenly as they had vanished, one night they reappeared! As if from nowhere. As far as I was concerned this had proven once and for all that this phenomena is not only real, but being coactive with us.

Back to ectoplasm. This energy was faked in many Victorian pictures because of the "Need" to prove the work of mediums to a suspicious public. Many mediums thought it would be ok to reenact seances for the camera, and stage these events.

The worst offender at the time was Helen Duncan whose "Cheese cloth up the nose" and "paper spirits" bore no resemblance to reality, and destroyed the opportunity of using photographs as evidence for many years. For the record ectoplasm or plasma is the word I would rather use bares no resemblance to cheese cloth or bed linen!

It is by nature a vapor composition, and mainly white in colour which is how the ghost as a bed sheet image has emerged over the years. I also think that the concept of ghosts being associated with lightning has some basis in reality. We already know that spirit rely on fluorescence, and use that to make themselves seen. Could we not assume that lightning creates the same effect? If it acted like a camera flash then it may well have made it possible see spirit…...If that makes sense

However, as I said these days we have to distance ourselves from the word ectoplasm because of these very associations and choose to use the word Plasma.

The common factor is that spirit energy require a host energy source to create plasma in order to manifest, either outside, as in the my picture of "Tatiana" (see pictures) for example, or inside of you, as in the case of transfiguration mediums, where a mediums face is seen to change into the recognisable form of a loved one. Either way plasma is the mutable substance that allows this to happen.

Plasma, often referred to as the forth state of matter, is basically a change from one composite form to another, as when water boils and becomes steam/

Using "concentrated Ion's" we can create three-dimensional images, such forms become visible as plasma forms (See my pictures), 99% of the universe exists in a plasma state. For example water molecules are made up of atoms. Each atom contains a balanced number of protons (positive charges) and neutrons (|Negative charges). Therefore the atom has a neutral charge.

If we add heat energy to solid water, the molecules speed apart and we get gas, add even more energy and the electrons are ripped right out of the atoms. And that leaves a mixture of free-floating electrons and atoms, which now have a positive charge (since the electron balance has now gone).

So typically plasma is a mixture of electrons and positive ions. The product of this is usually a brilliant display of electrical energy like fire (See pics) this is real plasma by its very nature.

Plasma "excreted" by spirit is the next expected photographic evidence that usually comes after photographing orbs. Mutable, it will often form into the shape of the consciousness creating it. (Again see the pics especially the one of Tatiana)

However spirit don't just rely on that to reveal themselves, or indeed just move things around or make bangs using Chi or Ki, no they are great manipulators of reflective light.

Essentially plasma, like orbs reacts to fluorescence, and spirit use light to manifest for the camera. Reflective light is especially available to them, so mirrors, TV's, glass, like windows patios ETC can be intelligently manipulated or "morphed " to create an image, usually of themselves.

I remember a case where I was called out to a house in Shoreham about two hours from where I live because the family, or particularly, the lady of the house had convinced herself that her brand new Plasma TV was haunted by the former owner of the house.

In reality it was she who was the source of this being, sensitive as it were, and had gone to the lengths of throwing this brand new TV out on to the dump, (The very thought broke my heart,)! She sighted the reason as being that she could see the face of the former house owner on the screen when the TV was off.

I told her that if she was going to throw away her TV to try and stop this she would also have to remove every mirror in the house, every piece of glass or door, in short anything that might reflect light.

My most famous picture to date is the one that appears of the priest giving last rites with this "Disembodied" arm which was "reflected " in glass. My first assumption had been that there was a picture opposite or something like that reflecting the image off the glass, there of course was not, and as the management assured me, never had been.

When investigating something of this nature, the one thing that I struggle to get across to people is that "Orbs" are not evidence of a haunting. I have in the past received any amount of calls from people who want me to investigate their property, usually a pub or hotel, based on the fact that they had photographed Orbs there.

Orbs are more likely associated with type A manifestations, and so closely linked to the platform style of communication. In other words they are friends or family members and as such I see them as part of our lives wherever we go, and tend to link to people not places.

So consequently I have disappointed a lot of people because in truth pictures of Orbs are not enough to state a place is haunted. After the publicity I got from the media during a couple of investigations I have to say that I also became very dubious as to whether people were looking for a media ride for their Pub or Hotel.

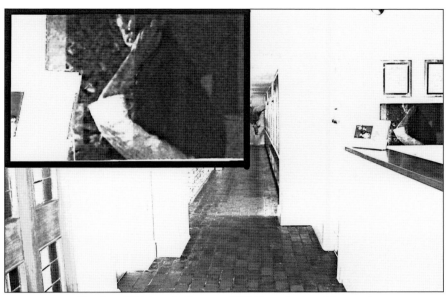

Star inn. Alfriston. Halloween 2008 'the priest and the arm'

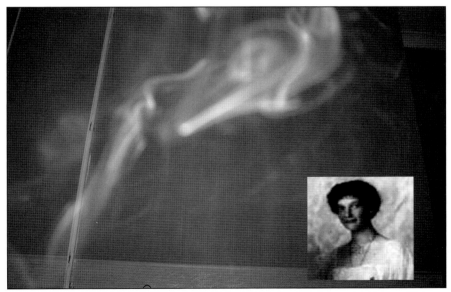

The apparition of Tatiana Romanov. Christmas 2007.

Calling orbs

Orbs arriving by "asking"

"Face" by the sofa

Casper at Christmas!

Ocean bowling (tweedie)

Orbs in the West Country

Mike with Robin Lown

K2 in action

Huge crowd at the High Beech .

South East Today with Sharon Williams

Mike and Kim

CHAPTER SIX

"Investigating the impossible"

IT HAD BEEN a warm summer's day and I didn't expect much of a turn out at the Spiritualist church in Bexhill. However I was surprised to find a half-full church, which for a summers afternoon and a Wednesday at that was quite a surprise.

Prayers were said from the platform. Before I opened up to the spirit world and started offering messages. It was the last reading that afternoon, and the image of a young teenage lad came to my head, showing me his passing I was absolutely certain that he had passed himself over.

This information I passed onto the crowd, and offered them the name of ""Karl".

A lady in one of the aisles glanced at me seemingly in disbelief, and gingerly raised her hand.

"What do you understand of this"? I asked

"All of what you said, Karl was my step son"

"He's talking about "Sean " I said

"That's his brother" She said in astonishment (although Stephen had been his other brother and the one he was closest to. There is no explanation I can offer for this other than the fact that maybe he had tried to say Stephen and I didn't hear)!

Karl went on to tell me all about his passing and how after his dad had hacked down the tree that he had used to take his life. He tried to place the nature of how he felt in my head at the time, the emotion behind it was very strong. You felt it yourself so that can be kind of hard to take on board.

Her name was Pam, and later that day, after the session when we all retired to the upstairs room for a cup of tea and a biscuit, explained that she had tried to hear from Karl for the last few years but attempts had not been successful.

In a letter to me she wrote.

"Michael, I would have hastily given you the keys to my car, and my house for everything you told me. I had waited five years to hear from Karl, and no one else managed to do what you did. You are the best in your field".

She later said that she had become tried of ambiguity from the platform, and the generalisations in churches and had decided that day not to go again if she hadn't heard anything.

Like many of the people I have read for over the years She stayed in touch, or would say Hi if she saw me in the street. On one-occasion yeas later she came bounding up to me in Tesco's

We got talking and she told me that she was now one of the managers at "Ocean Bowling" in Bexhill. My ears pricked up because my girlfriend at the time, now my wife, Kim was looking for a job So I asked Pam if there was anything going.

I don't think Kim thanked me for it because the job was cooking in the diner, and lasted all through a very hot summer with no weekends off, but it did us a turn while Kim found her feet again down south after living in Scotland for a number of years.

However her time at Ocean bowling was to prove to be memorable for so many reasons. Notwithstanding the friendship we got from Pam, and the friends we made there, including the part Owner Ash, who himself has sadly passed into the spirit world now.

Ocean Bowling came into the reckoning because for a while a number of staff had experienced various strange phenomena including hearing voices when they were alone including Knockings, seeing fleeting images coupled with the feeling of being watched, or even having something placed down and moved moments later.

It is worth mentioning that there were some members of staff who experienced nothing at all and thought it was all a load of Pooh!.

As I have said before strong E.M.F's can give the illusion of a haunting because they effect the brain, and cause you to feel all of these things. So therefore if you can find a physical reason for this haunting then we might have to conclude that its not, but just in the wrong location!

However, that said, an initial sweep of the area proved that there was nothing out of the ordinary and so encouraged me to investigate further.

I asked Colin Fuller again from the Hastings spiritualist church to join me with his wife, and my then girlfriend and now wife Kim, who herself is blessed with remarkable mediumistic ability.

We brought with us an array of equipment, including two infa red sensitive camera's, 4. E m f detectors, two laser thermometers, and a number of digital voice recorders.

We were joined by various staff members, including Pam herself who had experienced some of the reported goings ONS.

After closing we separated into two groups, and tried to form a state of mind that would allow for suitable communication with any connecting energy.

Straight away a member of staff called Phil started to take pictures of orbs. If anything it at least showed us that he had some rapport with sprit. As I said this is not proof of a haunting, but I did take on board that there was an unusually high amount of spirit emanations around him.

I have to confess that as a medium I have never found it easy to link to any residual energy or spirit that holds the earth plane (Type A), when going to the said locations I have opened myself up, but found the links to be of Type B in origin, In other words the friends and family of the people I was with.

So all credit to the mediums on "Most Haunted", however, in this case I was staggered to get the strong impression of a man whose image actually made me go cold. The reason being was that he was hooded!

Now, if you were, even in day light walking down the road, and you saw say a black monk with the hood up, and no discernable facial features, would than not give you the creeps? Well you can imagine how I felt!

It was at times like this when I really hoped it was my imagination or paradolia (Paradolia is where the brain tries to create a recognisable image),

But in this instance I could even hear a voice. It was saying something like "I'm' not going, you can't make me go" It was at that point I was fortunate to be given a name, "Tweedie"

So I allowed our minds to fuse for no other reason that to allow communication I hasten to add, I became aware that this black earth bound form had been there for good and sound reasons long before the building was.

There were 12 of us altogether. I think it was eleven of us who squeezed into a back room and asked Tweedie to join us. All of us witnessed this black hooded figure step out of the shadows and stand in front of us.

One of the former managers, a girl called Amber seemed to be the particular focus of his attention, and Tweedie started to talk about her. This I heard as part of my mediumship skills rather than a disembodied voice. He went on to say that he knew "This girl" and that she had started coming here at 14 years of age and that she had worked in the bar before working on the actual bowling. These facts she confirmed, but did not seemed phased by this attention. It is worthy of mention that in the photograph taken of him, it is Amber in the picture that he chooses to show himself on. Moments later a similar picture with another girl "Danni" shows no sign of Tweedie at all.

Twelve of us also witnessed a glass move all on its own. That is on its own. No fingers on, literally on its own. The trouble is this being the first investigation of this kind for me I expected all the others to be the same. I didn't realize that I was just lucky. Nearly all the investigations I have done since have yielded absolutely nothing at all.

Colin prepared what we call a clearing, and we opened up a doorway which we felt Tweedie had passed into, Or is that what he wanted us to think ??? In any case things have now quieted down at ocean bowling and they have been able to get on with their lives.

So to a degree I really began to appreciate the event at ocean Bowling, for me it was a first.

I went on to do a clairvoyant night at the Best Western Royal Victoria hotel with Colin and after a man called Mark Wey approached me, who was middle management at the Eastbourne waterworks. He asked me to take a look as a number of staff were complaining of the SOME kind of things going on like at Ocean bowling, so obviously I was more than happy to.

We went down on a Saturday night and set up the equipment. This proved to be the most fascinating experiment of all, but unfortunately for poor Mark opened up a Pandora's box of media hype that neither of us were prepared for.

The story of the investigation literally went worldwide. Even now I struggle to think of a country that didn't pick up on it, and report it. I did interviews around the globe, and was firmly kicked in the crunches by the skeptical community in various publications.

We got some interesting pictures down there but nothing conclusive I'm afraid to say the reason being was that the links I got were known to the staff and as such not provably residual. There was a strong network of underground cables that produced the biggest natural E.M.F readings I had ever seen in my life, and based on what I have already said about what they can do to you was forced to conclude that although there was a higher than average amount of paranormal activity down there it was still inconclusive, in other words I didn't know!

Now, as I said this initiated a media storm of miss quotes and nonsense, up until that time If someone had for example denounced Most haunted as all fake, I would have assumed that they would have had some behind the scenes knowledge or some research/evidence to back these claims up. I now realise that people will say anything as an opinion whether its right or wrong, probably just for attention.

People will talk rubbish, and state opinion without knowing any facts or without wanting to know the truth. I now see this as an ego driven campaign and don't give public opinion much heed.

Even now on the Internet you can find headlines like ...

"Parapsychologist Michael Kingscote hoaxes sewer haunting! Of course I did nothing of the kind. I stated time and time again that the sewer haunting was not totally provable due to the natural flow of E.M.F's

The Sun newspaper reported that I was down the sewer trying to chase away a zombie, which encouraged blogs from people implying that I was stupid enough to be fooled by a tramp or hobo down there, one person posted a picture showing where the tramp had got in, only problem was that the sewer he showed in the picture was of one in The US, and certainly not Eastbourne.

I was invited onto a Internet related radio podcast, and was interviewed by a softly spoken American from Louisiana called Brian, a confirmed skeptic known as the "Amateur scientist"

I got the impression from him that no matter what I said; he was there to debunk it, even when I thought I was actually agreeing with him!

I of course adopted the standpoint I have tried to take as much as possible in this book, that everything in it must also have a scientific basis or backing and felt that

I had an answer for every question that he threw at me, and as some of these answers had undergone scientific scrutiny, I did not understand why it was that he was so reluctant to take on board what we know are provable facts. I can only evoke A.D.S syndrome again!

I thought that I was agreeing with him when I explained how natural E.M.F's can effect the temporal lobe and cause the feelings of being haunted rather than there actually being a haunting. I sighted the huge network of cables underground as a possible cause for these feelings, and thought we would be on the same page.

You know he tried to debunk it. He actually questioned that if this were the case why don't factories have this too. ? Well actually they do, the waterworks in terms of size is far greater than any landmass a factory would take up, especially in terms of cabling.

One of the issues that Brian took up with me which itself is quite interesting was why it was that when people have a sitting, for example, a ouija board, nothing happens unless you say had your fingers on a glass, funnily enough it didn't move when you took your fingers off!

Obviously he was implying it was only because people were pushing it, though I have tried to explain as we went along here the random Ki principles.

" A good point" I replied, "accept that in the very first investigation (ocean bowling), twelve people did in fact witness a glass move by itself, in a state of continuence, just after everyone had removed their fingers from it.

(I have also saw a glass hit an investigative journalist, and a table move across a room during a circle).

After the said investigation, skepticism reigned supreme, and people expressed this in the media, and the letters page of the local rag. I also had the Christian fraternity attack me in the paper claiming that I had no knowledge, did not know what I was doing, and that spirits cannot communicate from the dead. Etc

So I accepted an offer to go on local radio to try and put the record straight. I am not a liar. I may be many things but a liar is not one of them, so I sometimes find it hard to be called that, and a con man even more. I have never understood why people were questioning my word because for me I never felt I had given anyone reason to. Sure I made mistakes, even trying the old multi level marketing stuff, but that was done in innocence.

So when I was asked to investigate " The mermaid" In Bexhill, I took sovereign radio, and Sharon Williams with me. As you may recall she had been the person I had read for prior to the Winter Gardens event. She had obviously become very interested in what I had done, and wanted to experience the kind of validation that I had experienced for herself, and luckily she wasn't to be disappointed

The mermaid is it is now known, was its original name though when we called in it was called "The Mistral" bar. Located on the Bexhill seafront it has a worthy history that goes back to its Edwardian roots. They had been having a few experiences, though not particularly negative, but wanted some definition as to what they were dealing with, and maybe just a little assurance.

Just as soon as we were shown around, I was able to link to a spirit energy that resided there. As I explained before this was not my forte, and usually found it easier to link to family members. While this was going on I set up the range of equipment that I had available to try and gather proof. I had Kim, Sharon, with Phil Standel Originally from Ocean Bowling, and Sally, who also worked at the bowling alley at the time, but was now the new owner, and I also invited Mark and Kelly Wey from the Eastbourne Waterworks.

Sharon brought recording equipment with her so that we would be able to broadcast our findings, but sadly it being radio and not TV we had to rely on audio.

We did record a moment during a traditional sitting. A glass evidently "Threw" itself at Sharon and landed on her lap this moment was recorded and eventually played on "South east today".

As a result of this success I was asked by Sovereign to do something for Halloween in and around the Eastbourne area, and after knocking on doors and begging, agreed with two places for a double venue gig on Halloween dividing the time between The Priory Court Hotel, and the old law courts in Pevensey.

For me an agreement is binding, that is the way I choose to live my life, and expect that off others, so was sad that both venues pulled out at the last minute.

However I found the Star Inn at Alfriston more than willing to step in, and proved itself to be the ideal replacement for the latter two venues.

The Inn itself goes back to the 13th century and had a huge history of smugglers, and even had the odd scattering of Monks here and there.

On the initial meeting, Kim and I went there to meet the manager, who I have to say was exceptionally helpful; She gave us a tour and Kim asked if she could take a few pictures.

We were little prepared for what this random effort was to have in store for us. When we later looked at the snaps we just stared in disbelief. There appeared to be in a reflected image, a man standing there, and what appeared to be a disembodied arm stroking his face.

We came to know this as "the priest" picture cause it looked very much like a last rites, as the arm had to be from someone lying down. You can clearly see arthritis in the fingers and knuckles. This was hugely exciting for us and it filled Halloween 2008 with great expectations

We were joined By Sharon Williams and Simon Rose from sovereign FM. Simon had to do the breakfast show so didn't stay all night. The idea had been to broadcast a Live feed from the hotel, but for whatever reason none of the equipment would work when we got there.

Although we didn't get anything as graphic as that picture, light anomalies were seen to be following Simon as he went around the building

As part of the investigation we gathered at the sight of the photograph we had taken the week before and tried everything possible to debunk the picture. This we did by trying to recreate it in every shape and form, even by hanging Sharon on her side to try and place her arm in the same position as the woman's in the picture. We rapidly concluded that it could not be done.

Simon Rose, a former photographer had been very pleased with the pictures, and although skeptical, could not debunk them in any way,

The pictures aside we also had plenty of personal experiences that night. Personal experiences are not generally regarded as evidence because they are largely in the eye of the beholder. One of these moments involved all of us at the same time when we were in different parts of the building.

I had taken myself off to the "heritage room" about 2am when without warning I heard a sigh in my ear. It was very loud, exaggerated. Almost as if you were signing to be sarcastic if that makes sense?

I rushed downstairs to tell Kim and Sharon what had just happened, and before I could get a word in they both told me that just moments ago they had simultaneously experienced the same thing. A major "Sigh" in the ear!

Within the hour we had once more started to walk around and experienced a stone being thrown across the floor. What was interesting was that I had talked to Kim earlier about this sort of thing always happening in Most haunted, and had poured scorn on it, and now it had actually happened.

The only other thing re investigations of this nature would be my very (small) part in "Bryony makes a zombie movie"

The sun newspaper had picked up on the Eastbourne waterworks, as I previously said, reporting that there had been a zombie in the sewer, so I was now the zombie hunter!

At the time You tube sensation Byony Matthewman had announced that she was going to make an on-line zombie movie using participants from all over the world to make the first movie of this nature

I was contacted by Hattrick productions for BBC3 who decided to actually make a documentary of this. (Who says the license fee is a waste of money)!!!

Up until now Bryony had been best known for her Amy Winehouse and Brittany Spears impressions on you tube, which had netted her millions of hits (Literally)

The BBC had the idea of making a small portion of the documentary during a ghost hunt at the "horse and groom" in Enfield.

On the day, Bryony showed up only at the conclusion of most of the filming in true pre-Madonna style, and then refused to participate other than a short sultry interview that was staged. Sadly this was cut from the programme in the end, mainly due to the fact that this was about her and she wouldn't have been in it!

The beeb made a version of it and put it on You- tube, somehow managing to condense three hours into four minutes.

The result of this mini- doc is a bit of fun, and not to be taken seriously. As for the whole making an Internet zombie movie thing, well, it never really happened. It didn't help that Bryonny , again in true pre -Madonna style decided it was more important to take a holiday to America at the crucial moment rather that try and see this through. Shame really because this girl had all the makings of being a famous TV celeb, but the attitude of a Hollywood star.

CHAPTER SEVEN

"Spiritualism vs orthodoxy and the great Bible debate"

THERE HAVE been many incidents over the years of infamous clashes between what I describe as orthodox Christian and Christian Spiritualist. I have spent hours debating the issue with every kind of Christian sect from Jehovah's witnesses to Mormons.

The only difference between them and me as I can see, as an individual that I respect them far more than they respect me. This is a fact.

If they are happy in their belief system, then I am happy for them, and would not try and change that providing they were not knowingly harming someone, then its all good. One thing I do believe in is the exploitation of free will. Our choices in life are what shape us.

I will say that to date, no one has ever convinced me that any of these versions of mainstream Christian Orthodoxy is right, and in so being, I was wrong in what I do.

The main source of the argument is the way in which the Bible is interpreted, and the literal interpretation people seem to make of the text. Defense of the texts presented as a literal understanding I think are down (Again) to A.D.S (Auto defence system)

How do I know? Because I had it myself

Many years ago when I was at College, and its worth mentioning that at the time I had not been to church, or was even following my path as was expected of me after my confirmation, despite all of this something occurred that really made me sit back and think.

During one of the lessons the discussion opened up to religion, and one of my good friends at the time from both School and college Phillipe Shaw ended up by saying something along the lines of "Well Christianity is just another religion, its no different to all the others!

My reaction still shocks me to this day. Normally quiet, not being the brightest one there I tended to keep in the background, I found myself aroused with my hackles into command central!

"You can't call Christianity just a religion, it's not the same. It's the reality, in comparison everything else is just a bogus form of worship"

His reaction was just to laugh "prove it then" he said with his familiar shoulder jump. Of course I couldn't. The only explanation for my defense at the time was "because it says so in the Bible" etc etc at which he just laughed!

As the years passed I realised that I had A.D S which meant that no matter what people said, I had displayed an inability to be objective. I went to the defense mode against anything that would compromise my belief system.

This I have found to be the case with any who now challenge my understanding of life after death based on biblical interpretation, most offered to me is that argument that I don't talk to spirit, but I, being fooled by the Devil, or some form of demonic influence.

The first thing I notice is the way in which such quotations are cited as fact despite there being no evidence other than an individual interpretation of scripture. For example John W Milor, in his book "Aliens in the Bible" goes as far as to state as a fact that " Spirit guides are not guides at all but demons"

I would have been more interested in Milor's credibility had he said just three simple words "In My opinion". This to me would have been worth a tonne of gold, but to state something, as fact without some form of scientific scrutiny is in fact very arrogant, as there is no support for this statement other than an interpretation of events in scripture.

The whole of his book works on the angle of the new age turn around who discovers Jesus and then denounces everything extraneous to that belief. His book deliberately plays down facts with regards to new age understanding in order to increase the credibility behind his beliefs.

In order for Milor to be right we would have to accept that scripture is 100% accurate, and the historical facts are that it is not and that is a fact that cannot be altered by any amount of belief. Now don't get me wrong here. I am not knocking the existence of God, or even Christ, What I am saying is that The Bible has been shown to be inaccurate in both historical accuracy, and geography.

As I understand it, the texts which evoke the pro Christian, anti spiritualist argument are based on the fact the version of the Bible we have today is what we call the Pauline version. Had it not been separated from its Gnostic counterpart, we would also be celebrating reincarnation as part of this belief system as well as communication with spirit.

In fact Theologists suggest that the literal interpretation of the resurrection was placed by the then leader of the church, Bishop Iraneus in response to a fear of Gnosticism.

The main gospels namely, Matthew, Mark, Luke and John, according to Iraneous were selected because they were known to Christ at the time, and therefore were the most accurate. We know that this simply is not true. These Gospels were written and presented between 50 and two hundred years after the death of Christ. In fact the Gnostic texts date earlier.

So what are the Gnostic gospels?

Here are the thirty or more gospels that originally were part of the Bible, and were removed or separated at a time when the church was taking control, and Rome now used the one thing it had tried to destroy in order to create power. Christianity. Now if the literal interpretation of the resurrection of Christ was in anyway compromised, then so was the power because it had to be total.

Therefore any reference to spirit communication or rebirth could not be included in these religious texts and so were removed! Period!

Gnostic Christians at the time did not accept the physical resurrection. In fact even in orthodox texts the references challenge this.

For example when Saul (Paul) met Jesus, He is not shown to be a person in a physical body, but a spiritual energy. Where orthodoxy cleaves to its belief in the resurrection is where Jesus is known to walk around, and display his body after the crucifixion, especially to Thomas whom he asks to touch his wounds.

The Gnostic gospels challenge this, and even the gospel of Mary suggests that this event was related from a dream.

I am not trying to knock the resurrection, just the way we understand it. At the end of it all, if this was the case, there were no spirit, and we were being fooled by demons, then even in the Pauline version of events can we explain the transfiguration, where Jesus speaks to Moses and Elijah?!!!!!!!!!!

The fact remains that scripture has been edited by man for man from Iraneus to Clement of Alexandria, and the council of Nicea in the 12th century. And all with one aim, to use Christianity to control, and I'm sorry if this offends but these are facts known to historians and theologians for centuries, and totally trash the concept created by those you would diminish spirituality by continually hacking on that we are products of Satan's work, and are being fooled by him. This day and age the destructiveness of this argument needs to be addressed.

As for Milor, his arguments against us are weak. We already know of the dangers and destructiveness Ouija boards can cause. And this book has gone along way to agree with that statement, and explain why. If you take anything from this you will know that we as people are good and bad, and that nothing changes immediately, not even on the other side.

Were we to follow orthodoxy literally we would be in a lot of trouble. For example Deuteronomy Chapter 17 Vs "-6 says "If anyone in a town is evil in the sight of God for serving other Gods, he must be stoned to death"

Now this begs the question that if we are indeed to take the Bible as a literal tool, this suggests that if anyone exercises the right of freewill, they should be punished for it?

Similar texts can also be found in Leviticus. It is also stated that we should stone to death a teenager who is rebellious. (Ok that's not such a bad idea)!!and also tells us its ok to have slaves. It also tells us that if a woman is raped its her fault for not putting up a strong enough struggle..

Corinthinans 14-34

"As in all the churches of the saints the woman should keep silent in the churches, for they are not permitted to speak but should be subversive as even the law says if there is anything they deserve to know let them ask their husbands"

Well ok, it's starting to win me over now! But seriously, if we had taken that literally where would we be right now? And I can't imagine any of the women I have known in my life remaining that humble. My point is this, in that we have had to allow room for interpretation. And we cannot be selective as to where those borders are.

So when science meters out facts because we as a race have managed somehow to evolve, we need to stop with the ancient demonics and move on as we cannot and will not evolve!"

Interestingly this brings to mind the biblical stories of "Theckra" whose that???

Theckra is a heroine of the Bible whose story was removed for no other reason than the fact that she was a woman

There are a number of "Miracles" associated with the story of Theckra, her story being of one who rose from slavery to martyr.

Again all I am trying to say is that literal interpretations have bogus origins. In the beginnings there were two fractions of Christianity, and if the Gnostic version had been the one we live our lives around, then I would not be writing this today.

Many of the texts in the Bible still demonstrate an essence of this. Many texts can be compared to Buddhists texts, which at the time predated Christianity by some 300 years.

This added weight to the feeling people had that Jesus spent time in the east as a youth, and so was influenced by these Buddhist teachings. According to legend, he was after all visited at his birth by three "people" from the east.

In reality, science is now the way forward to hopefully reprieve our Christian values/ if by the validations, especially in quantum theory we can all find a place on the earth to be without belief conflict then we have found the ideal world. But this has to be down to science or nothing is ever going to change.

What appeals to me about this particular blend of faith referred to as spiritualism is that in these churches literally anyone of any faith is welcome. This cannot be said of other mainstream branches of Christianity. It always makes me laugh how in the Bible itself, Christ is condemned for casting out devils, because according to his accusers it is in the name of the devil that he a casts out the devil. Funny really. Nothing much has changed in the last 2000 years.

If this were true, that we sit in the light, draw in the light, pray to the light in the name of Christ, and evoking our God only to have Satan show up then the whole 2000 years have been a mockery, notwithstanding the crucifixion itself.

For an accurate portrayal of those times I would refer to the historian Flavius Joespheus, and his famous book "Antiquities of the Jews" who is considered by most to have presented the most accurate understanding of life in the region, at the time of Christ. More accurate because this was during that lifetime, not two or even three hundred years after.

Because of the existence of texts from the time, many that were only discovered during the last war at Nag Hammadi, we now know that even geographical structures were not accurately portrayed, and wonder if language translations holds the key to these problems. For example even the word Jesus itself is Greek, and would not have been known at the time. The various interpretations of that name would have been Yesu or Yesuha. And Nazareth may not even have existed. It has become more apparent that Nazareth would have come many years later and maybe named after the savior, rather than being the place of the saviour.

If that's the case where does the word Nazareth come from? Well in all likelihood it would be from the word Nazreon which meant rabbi or teacher!

Again I would just like to say that I am not knocking faith. Just some criticism aimed at the way I have chosen to live my life based on really common sense! And if you choose to ignore common sense, then the Bible is very clear about what we should do to people who work on the Sabbath. They must be stoned to death! I'll meet you all at Tesco's next Sunday. Bring your own stones!

Before I leave this contentiousness alone and close the door on it so I can move on, I would just like to briefly mention something that has been talked about a lot over the last few years. This is the possibility that Jesus did not die on the cross, but survived and eventually moved to Kashmir where he died, living into old age.

The evidence for this is as well endorsed as the evidence against it. For me, It does not matter either way as again; quantum physics has proved how we tailor our belief system to suit us.

This means that if we see Christ as a Blue eyed Geoffrey Hunter or Robert Powell, then that is who will greet us. In other words we fashion the quantum field, we take what we have made Christ to be.

In the last 2000 years its this that makes him powerful, and elevates him to the Godhead, not the events that surrounded his life all those years ago. It's the mind essence that has created the power that holds us together and protects us, and made even his name sacred. This will not change.

CHAPTER EIGHT

"Basic mediumship development"

ISN'T ebay BRILLIANT? Only a few days ago Kim was perusing the site for a potential bargain, and it seems only a moment later Arthur Conan Doyle's book of the beyond had been pushed through our letterbox. My how modern technology has moved on, and at such a rapid pace?

The reason I feel drawn to mention this is that within its pages I noticed an illustration of various levels appertaining to be various levels/dimensions in the spirit world. It goes on to explain how we live within one level on the other side and progress to higher dimensions in effect dying all over again.

Well this is of course not unlike not only what I have discovered to be the case through personal understanding, but again, let me draw on quantum physics and how we appear to be making our own reality, and in a macabre way, its own validation of life after death,

Because of quantum physics we have been able to understand and learn more about mediumship than ever before, and bring exactly what mediumship is down to its basic components. This now presents the argument of how much do we really need to have to sit in mediation to be mediums when quantum physics explains it in a far more basic context.

As a development still further of the mediumship process, people have claimed to be able to predict the future. The first name that comes to mind has to be Nostrodamus.

To this day many hold his predictions in the highest regard, but we also have to be open minded to the fact that many times his information has been ambiguous, and in reality, if you are not making a reference to a specific year and time, say down to a month the chances are it can be made to fit.

It's a bit like the Bible code. This in essence seems like a fantastic revelation where texts when processed through a simple computer system appear to be showing specific references to current affairs. However the fact remains that if you pick any text (Moby dick was used) then a similar success has been noted.

That said, quantum physics takes us outside the space time continuum, to the degree that if for arguments sake we were to believe in reincarnation, we would now refer to these past lives of ours as other lives rather than making a specific reference to the past or future. This is because outside of space time there would be no past or future. For that reason alone I would have to say that yes it is possible to predict the future. You just have to find a way to lock into the unconscious in a way that we effect our own quahtum field.

If we are in effect creating our own reality as we go. Bare in mind quantum particles are not matter until they are observed, then we are almost creating that future!

Quantum theory tells us that every time we have a single thought we go into a world of possibilities. One of these being that every time we have a thought we are creating a new reality. So a day will create hundreds of alliterative alternate situations and possibilities that we could potentially fall into

As for predictions, yes its possible. Quantum theory prove that as we create this reality we will leave little clues, so by going to a palmist or tarot reader you will receive a personal reading because a way of tapping into the Quantum consciousness which has already been arranged by you. Like leaving hundreds of little clues in a movie about who the villain is at the end.

By doing this we are getting in touch with the "universal feel" which is not like mediumship as that is the opinion of spirit. This is connecting with the universe, or that collective. And tells it like it is without opinion. This is what some call synchronicity. Things being meant to be because the journey was already mapped. Quantum physics proves it now as we enter a new phase, and a new wave of knowledge that starts with the Age of Aquarius but goes nuts from 2012!

I remember many years ago wanting to move house. I needed a bigger place for the family, but needed peace and quiet to. I had a dream that night. I saw in this dream the perfect house. I even remember its number at the time, for arguments sake lets call it 452. The name was Althelstone rd, and it was backed onto some hills right next to a bungalow with iron railings running round.

The next day one set of property details arrived from the agents. It was of the same number, the same road, and the description was the same. As luck would have it I had told my ex wife what I had seen so had a witness to validate this. I was so excited I actually rushed to her place of work to show her the details and she could not believe her eyes.

Now what would you have thought had you made such an accurate prediction? That you were going to get the house? Yes so did I but someone else bought it!

So be warned, predictions are not always what they seem, liken them to a spider walking across the table. You can see what it does as you have an over all view point, but the spider does not have the sense or view point that we have to know that if it doesn't stop walking across the table soon its just going to fall of.

We can see it happening. Put money on it, but at the last minute the spider might just walk along the ridge.

So this is what separates being a spiritualist medium from being a palmist or tarot reader. All worthy causes and arts in there own right of course. I would in some cases send people to my good friend, palmist Robin Lown rather than send them to a counselor sometimes.

As a consultant member of the British Astrological and psychic society I would stress that my discipline is mediumship. Other members of the society might be readers of different kinds, but I have only been tested in mediumship.

Being a member of B.A.P.S does not make you an expert on every aspect of psychic research.

I developed mediumship over a long period of time, and get a little aggravated at being misquoted when I say I can show people how to be able to read, and even give a message from platform after just one day at one of my workshops. I have not now, or have I ever claimed that you would then be a medium, just that the understanding of what needs to be done and what is expected of you would be there.

During the start of a day's workshop I would start by exploring various things, most of which I have mentioned in this book already. The difference between sprits, Ghosts, residual energy, Type A, Type B etc, and the difference between mental and physical mediumship.

I also speak a lot about "Vritiis" a word that I mentioned earlier. This is a yogi expression that explains that, yes, spirit implant thoughts straight into your head, but sometimes when they leave, we can mistake our own thoughts for theirs!

In fact 75% of mediumship is done in this way. I have always said that on average a spirit can only hold the vibration near to ours for around twenty minutes. Experience has shown me that if it is going to go wrong, then it will be after around twenty minute!

So the first thing I say is that everything must be limited to twenty minutes with a view to avoiding Vrittis. Whether we are using dowsing, Ouija, or direct thought mediumship. Stop after twenty minutes. Spirit vibrations I liken to a helicopter blade that has to slow down to the same speed as ours when they work with us. The pull back to their real vibration will often result in those blades inadvertently speeding up when you least want them to!"

The greater part of mediumship in the early days involves just knowing when spirit are there and when they are not, because being a medium means simply inviting the energy to share the consciousness with us.

So with this in mind I believe in all honesty that there is no great secret to mediumship. No great wonder. We simply first evoke prayer and protection. I spent nearly all my young life in church and very early on learned to appreciate God, and love the name of Jesus as a name that evokes love and protection.

Remember I have not knocked "Jesus", only the truth of some aspects of his life, and the Bible as a source of accurate history telling.

So for 20 mins and 20 mins only we ask spirit to draw close. This is done simply by sending the thought out in love and light and the protection of the heavenly father. Then, we say "For the next twenty minutes the first thoughts we get are to be from spirit, second to our own" this in effect has invited spirit into our aura and given permission to share the consciousness.

All thoughts and feelings should then be noted. Don't be surprised if some of these do seem a little negative, spirit have to learn to work with us to, and also need to gage our reactions and see how strong we are if they are to work with us.

After the 20 mins, we must reverse this. We need to take charge, and avoid being continuously "Open"! So we say "From now on the first thoughts are ours, and ours alone!

Some people, particularly in the early days think that its cool to be walking along and giving messages off all the time. Not only will they end up having a nervous break down, but also unsolicited messages are wrong on so many levels and are usually not accurate anyway.

I call it "Don't eat mushrooms" syndrome because the first time it happened to me was after dem in Hailsam when a girl pointed a finger at me and "said "don't eat mushrooms". Of course I did and have been ever since to prove her wrong.

When opening or closing it may help to picture the chakra in your head opening and closing accordingly. See that as like camera shutters opening and closing at will. So when you open up. In you minds eye, see this doorway reaching to it to the universe, and find that place where you want to be. See the light pour in through that open chakra, and feel its warmth. When closing. Make sure that door is sealed tight.

Like everything its about sticking to the rules and knowing where the line is.

"Final thoughts"

ONLY NOW has it been possible to unify what hitherto could never be brought together. Of course despite the facts, there will always be those who mistrust what we have discovered in these pages as well as anything factual. These people would have us believe that we did not go to the moon; the Titanic never sank, and maybe even that the world is flat. At some stage we have to learn where that line is to be drawn.

For the moment I just want to thank you for staying with me on this brief journey, and wish you all well on your own journeys. If this book has proven anything, then it's that all these journeys are the same one by the same person in the end anyway. So be nice!

I am including at the end the article I wrote for mercury magazine regarding the Grand Duchess Tatiana. She materialized in front of us at my home, and her picture is included. I hope you enjoy her story and her message from the grave.

Take care and God bless

Michael Kingscote.

"A Theory validated from the grave, from the grand Duchess Tatiana Romanov, the second daughter of the last Tsar"

AS A MEDIUM, one will accumulate many anecdotes over the years, one such anecdote that springs to mind personally comes from a demonstration of clairvoyance when a very sincere lady accused me of being an alien from another planet!

She may well be right about that, but my personal evidence for survival was a long way from that, and started back in 1995, when a lifetimes fascination was about to take a new and unexpected twist.

Since the age of 11, I had a fascination with the story of the lost princess, the Russian Anastasia, who had been the stuff of films and books for over fifty years.

Although there seemed evidence to support a claimant to be this princess, she had not been accepted, and I quite rightly wondered why?

I had first been drawn to the Romanov family from a picture in a book I had seen about Edward the Seventh. For some strange reason I had always been drawn to them.

I admit I did believe the claimant, who at the time was known as Anna Anderson, but later proved to be a polish factory worker called Franziska Schanscowska.

One Sunday I was at work when a strange set of circumstances was about to change my life forever. I had, the previous week, had strange visions of a tall slender girl. I had seen a wheel chair, and got the letters L and A in my head. Then I heard "Daughter of the Tsar".

This happened a number of times, but I failed in every attempt to get any more information, or understand what it was I was getting. This was made all the more curious as Anastasia had been short and dumpy, and this certainly was not she!

Then, on this Sunday, I realized I had brought the wrong paper by mistake, and had to settle for the Mail on Sunday, which I sometimes found a little heavy, although be assured, I like to think |I am a little distant from the Sunday sport!

As my folding machine ran I turned the pages to see a picture of a tall dark haired girl, and a face I recognized. This face had been the one in my visions, then second to that I saw the headline, is this the daughter of the Tsar who survived?

I remember going numb with excitement. As I read the article it pointed to a historian, Michael Occleshaw, and new book called "the Romanov conspiracies" which spoke of the theory that Tatiana, the second daughter of the Tsar had survived the family execution somehow, and had lived in a village in Kent.

The second coincidence came the following Friday when my father in law at the time, who had just had a hip replacement, offered me a book that he had purchased, I understand unintentionally. It was the Romanov Conspiracies.

I read it from cover to cover that night. It spoke of a rescue of this princess, and how she spent her last years living in the village of Lydd. Lydd in Kent is just over an hour's drive from Hastings where I live!

She had been known as Larissa (L .A)? And had spent her time in an old fashioned bath chair until her death due to T B and spinal caries in 1926

Shocked and stunned, I knew she had made contact with me from beyond the grave, the only question was why me?

With this in mind I had to speak to author Michael Occleshaw, but how was I to do this? "Hey, I'm a psychic medium, and I am just calling to say I know your right"???

No, this had to be handled gently, and also I would need more evidence, perhaps something that he had not put in his book. However, try as I might I could not get anything new, or worthy of mention. Maybe I was trying to hard, I don't know.

I needed to talk to him, not to mention the spiritual aspect, but maybe at first just to compliment the book? Of course the publishers would not give me his address, but agreed to forward any letter on my behalf, this they did, and I got a letter back which thrilled me to the core.

Then after a period of time I wrote again, still not being forward regards my mission, but talking about plays and film ideas. One was involving what might have happened had the Tsar gone to trial, which was what many wanted at the time.

Then, the author moved house, and I lost contact for a while. The contact we reestablished through the publisher, and I had a new address for Michael Occleshaw.

Then something happened in 1997. I had to go to Herne bay in Kent. I won't say why, let's just call it business. However Herne bay was where Michael Occleshaw just happened to be living My business concluded I found the house and waited anxiously outside in the hope someone might come out.

The it started, the voice in my head "Knock at the door, knock at the door" I tried, but I felt like a stalker, and just could not knock at the door.

I left and went home. One the way I stopped off brought some flowers, and took them to Tatiana's grave in Lydd where I lay them down by way of an apology.

Back home it was like a sigh through my whole body. I knew that we, that is Michael Occleshaw and I were supposed to meet, and that I had let all parties down. In all seriousness what could I do Knock on the door and say "Hi Tatiana's been talking to me"? I never imagined that a buttoned up historian would ever have been opened up to a spirit communication.

By the time I did have the courage to knock on the door, the author, and his wife had moved to Virginia in America. The reality was that whatever task had been given me from spirit, I had failed in.

A number of years later I was demonstrating at a hall In Bexhill when I read for this couple in the audience. Although the messages from their loved ones were readily accepted, I felt embarrassed as I felt they were slightly negative.

My embarrassment was made all the worse, when at the end do of the demonstration; my lift home was to be shared with this couple. My good friend Brian Marland drove, while I sat in the passenger seat, and the couple sat in the back. As we spoke the subject got onto portraits and paintings, and the lady, whose name I now know to be Betty, said that they had a picture of one of the Russian Grand duchesses.

Instinctively I knew that they were not talking about Anastasia, and although I was not sure, felt that it was either going to be Maria, or my visitor of many years ago Tatiana, it was Tatiana.

I asked them if they knew that Tatiana might have survived the massacre at Ekaterinburg, and was buried at Lydd.

The answer shook my world. The gentleman looked straight at me and said, "I know that for a fact, I am the one that discovered the body"

Michael Occleshaw discovered the body I said "Your Michael Occleshaw"

Can anyone possibly imagine how I felt? Michael, a fellow spiritualist, and his medium wife Betty Occleshaw, they are now my closest friends.

I still don't know why Tatiana thought we should be together, but she thought that we should be and was determined to do this

At one point we did visit her grave together, and she gave me two names. One was Headstom, which to date has never been found to have any significance, and the other was Malamar.

A year or so later Michael discovered a story from the time that suggested that Tatiana had been unofficially engaged. The name of the boy in question was Dimitri De Malamar

Coincidence? No the point is spirit effect us in so many ways. This example shows how they can help and intervene if we open our minds.

At the Christmas of 2007, Tatiana appeared to us in front of the camera. We had been asking her for a while if she would and when the energy was right she achieved this. In a plasma form her face can clearly be seen.

There has been a lot of controversy over the DNA evidence attributed to the so called bodies of the Romanov's that were apparently discovered at the Koptyaki woods in Eketerinburg. The DNA is supposed to prove that these bodies are indeed all of the Romanov's and that they are now accounted for.

This is not true.

I believe that the family that were murdered at the "House of special purpose" that night were not the family, but body doubles. This is due to validations uncovered in the Summers and Mangold book the file on the Tsar where a priest called to the house testified that the second family bore little resemblance to the Romanov's whom he had served earlier.

As regards the DNA I think the public is being duped. Separate tests done by an independent body made comparisons to the families DNA from a sample taken from The Tsarina's sister Elisabeth (Ella) this is what they reported …

Conclusion. Considering molecular and forensic inconsistencies the identity of the Eketerinburg remains has not been established. Our mtDNA haplotyoe results for Elisabeth provide yet another line of conflicting evidence regarding the identity of the Ekaterinburg remains

Bibliography/Further reading

The Orb project. Klaus Heinemann / Miceal Ledwith.
Beyond Photography by Katie Hall and John Pickering
How to hunt Ghosts by Joshua Warren
The Romanov Conspiracies by Michael Occleshaw
Aliens in the Bible by John W Milor
Hidden messages in water by Masuru Emoto
The True Power of water by Masuru Emoto
The works of Flavious Josephus by William Whiston
The Gnostic Gospels by Elaine Pagals

MANOR CREATIVE
Design Print Multimedia

YOUR ONE STOP SHOP

Sustainable design & print solutions from quality printers who care about the environment.

- Low alcohol printing
- Process-less plates
- Vegetable oil based inks

- Low Carbon initiatives
- Responsible print
- FSC & PEFC Certified
- Recycled papers

TREES FOR LIFE
Restoring the Caledonian Forest

ACORN
BS 8555

carbonclear

FSC
The mark of responsible forestry
TT-COC-002794
© 1996 FSC A.C.

PEFC
Promoting sustainable forest management
PEFC/16-37-577

MAY DAY

INVESTOR IN PEOPLE

Beyond Faith is not just another book offering nothing but faith for evidence of post mortem survival

Beyond faith looks past that and convincingly explores the unification of science and faith. From Quantum physics to electromagnetic fields the evidence shows us what truly lies beyond the grave.

Mike Kingscote is a consultant member of the British astrological and psychic society and has a qualification in parapsychology and 20 years experience as a medium.

Photo courtesy of Gemmaine Baughurst

www.michaelkingscote.co.uk,
psychicmichael@tiscali.co.uk
Cover concept by Natasha Kingscote

ISBN: 978-0-9561711-2-2

£6.50

9 780956 171122